ISRAEL

Lessons From The Holy Land

A Devotional Tour Of
The Land Where Jesus Walked

DEVOTIONALS BY ERIC ELDER
PHOTOGRAPHY BY KARIS & MAKARI ELDER

Israel: Lessons from the Holy Land is part of a series of
inspirational resources produced by Eric Elder Ministries.
For a boost in your faith anytime, please visit:
www.TheRanch.org

Special thanks to my wife, Lana, for her inspiration to take this
special trip to the Holy Land, and for her helpful insights and
thoughtful enhancements during the writing of these devotional
messages. Thanks also to our photographers for the trip, Karis
and Makari Elder, our worship leaders, Lucas Elder and Gary
Marini, our travel coordinator, Dan Bergey of Pilgrim Tours,
(www.pilgrimtours.com), our local Israeli guide, Pilar Blanco,
and the rest of the team who ventured out with us on this
expedition and who made it so enjoyable: Leanne Benner, Ron
Ballard, Josiah Elder, Craig Elder, Jeanette Gaylord, Makayla
Gaylord, Joe Gerstung, Esther Gondwe, and Wayne Pogue.

ISBN 978-1-931760-31-7

WELCOME TO ISRAEL!

On the pages ahead, I'd like to take you on a "devotional tour" of the Holy Land. My goal is to help bring the Bible to life in a way that you may have never experienced before. We're going to look at the places where Jesus walked and taught and ministered, as well as the places where many other famous stories from the Bible took place. I pray that these devotionals will not only give you a deeper appreciation for this land that "the Lord your God cares for" (Deuteronomy 11:12), but that it will help you to grow closer to Christ—and stronger in your faith in Him.

Eric Elder

We loved touring Israel and we loved capturing it in pictures so you could enjoy it, too. We hope that these pictures will show you not only sites of Israel, but also the heart of this wonderful country. While going to Israel in person is great, we hope that this book is the next best thing to being there!

Karis & Makari Elder

Above left: Eric Elder in Jerusalem. Above right: Makari Elder (left) and Karis Elder (right) on the Mediterranean coast. Cover image: A scroll lies unfurled at a re-creation of a synagogue in Nazareth.

Introduction

TURNING SAD ENDINGS TO NEW BEGINNINGS

There's a spot in Jerusalem where you can walk inside a tomb from the time of Christ. As you walk in, you can imagine what it must have been like for those who walked into Jesus' tomb on that first Easter morning, when the angels greeted them with these words:

"Do not be afraid, for I know that you are looking for Jesus, who was crucified. He is not here; He has risen, just as He said. Come and see the place where He lay" (Matthew 28:6).

To take a walk into the tomb with me and see it for yourself, take a look at the short video I've posted on the Internet at the link below.* Then read on to see why the story of what happened that first Easter morning is perhaps the most significant event that's ever taken place in the entire history of Israel.

What I love about the Easter story is that just when it looked like all hope was lost, God showed up and showed the disciples that the death of Jesus wasn't the end—it was just the beginning of something even better.

*Watch "The Garden Tomb" on the Internet at this link http://youtube.com/watch?v=3Yq-Qoh-Kbk

Facing page: A tomb in Jerusalem from the time of Christ that could even be the one in which He was buried. Above left and right: A sign and a trail lead visitors to the Garden Tomb.

Above and right: Trails and benches throughout the Garden Tomb make it a quiet place to remember the life, death, and resurrection of Christ.

In a matter of days, the disciples went from thinking that their hopes and plans and dreams for the future had been dashed forever, to seeing that God had bigger hopes and plans and dreams for them than they could have ever imagined!

You can almost see their faces light up as God opens their eyes to the truth. Watch what happens as Jesus reveals Himself to two of the disciples as they walk along the road:

Now that same day two of them were going to a village called Emmaus, about seven miles from Jerusalem. They were talking with each other about everything that had happened. As they talked and discussed these things with each other, Jesus Himself came up and walked along with them; but they were kept from recognizing Him.

He asked them, "What are you discussing together as you walk along?"

They stood still, their faces downcast. One of them, named Cleopas, asked Him, "Are you only a visitor to Jerusalem and do not know the things that have happened there in these days?"

"What things?" He asked.

"About Jesus of Nazareth," they replied. "He was a prophet, powerful in word and deed before God and all the people. The chief priests and our rulers handed Him over to be sentenced to death, and they crucified Him; but we had hoped that He was the one who was going to redeem Israel. And what is more, it is the third day since all this took place. In addition, some of

our women amazed us. They went to the tomb early this morning but didn't find His body. They came and told us that they had seen a vision of angels, who said He was alive. Then some of our companions went to the tomb and found it just as the women had said, but Him they did not see" (Luke 24:13-24).

Take a look at the disciples' faces when Jesus first walks up and starts talking to them. The Bible says, "They stood still, their faces downcast." I don't know how exactly Jesus was able to hide His true identity from them, but I do know that it's hard to see when our faces are downcast. But look at what happens as the story continues.

He said to them, "How foolish you are, and how slow of heart to believe all that the prophets have spoken! Did not the Christ have to suffer these things and then enter his glory?" And beginning with Moses and all the Prophets, He explained to them what was said in all the Scriptures concerning Himself.

As they approached the village to which they were going, Jesus acted as if He were going farther. But they urged Him strongly, "Stay with us, for it is nearly evening; the day is almost over." So He went in to stay with them.

When He was at the table with

them, He took bread, gave thanks, broke it and began to give it to them. Then their eyes were opened and they recognized Him, and He disappeared from their sight. They asked each other, "Were not our hearts burning within us while He talked with us on the road and opened the Scriptures to us?"

They got up and returned at once to Jerusalem. There they found the Eleven and those with them, assembled together and saying, "It is true! The Lord has risen and has appeared to Simon." Then the two told what had happened on the way, and how Jesus was recognized by them when He broke the bread (Luke 24:25 -35).

The disciples went from downcast to delighted, and as they did, their hearts began to burn within them. They were eager to learn everything they possibly could from this Man who was walking with them, so much so that they "urged Him strongly" to stay with them. Then, when Jesus took the

Right: A cat finds contentment at the Garden Tomb.

Above: Golgotha means "the place of the skull," leading some to think that this hill near to the Garden Tomb could have been the spot where Christ was crucified, with its skull-shaped eyes and nose.

bread, gave thanks, broke it and began to give it to them, their eyes were opened to the Truth. Even though Jesus disappeared in that moment, their excitement about what they felt didn't disappear. They got up at once and ran to tell the others the good news: This wasn't the end at all, but just the beginning of something new!

There are times when you may feel like God, or people, or life itself has pulled the rug out from under you. It may seem like all your hopes and plans and dreams are crashing down around you. You might wonder how you'll ever be able to get back up again. But I want to encourage you to do what the disciples did as they walked along the road. They stopped looking down and they started looking up. They looked up to the One who held their life in His hands—the same One who holds your life in His hands—the One who gives each one of us "life and breath and everything else" (Acts 17:25b).

What may look like an ending to something in your life may in fact be just the beginning of something entirely new, something even bigger and better and more remarkable than you ever could have imagined. And if you think that's just wishful thinking, just remember the Easter story, and remember the God who specializes in turning sad endings into new beginnings!

Let's pray...

Father, thank You for the reminder that You can take the sad endings in our lives and turn them into new beginnings. Open my eyes that I may see just what you have in store for me. In Jesus' name, Amen.

**Below: A sign on the door to the Garden Tomb lets visitors know what they won't find inside.
Right: Inside the tomb, where the body would have lain.**

Lesson 1

WHERE DID ISRAEL GET ITS NAME?

On the pages ahead, I'd like to take you on a "devotional tour" of the Holy Land. In each lesson, I'll be asking (and answering) a question about Israel and some of the major events that have taken place there. My goal is to give you both a history lesson and a faith lesson: a history lesson about this land that is so precious to God, and a faith lesson that you can apply to your own life today.

I'd like to start with a foundational question: "Where did Israel get its name?"

To check your answer, keep reading on, or take a look at the short video clip at the link below that I recorded on the coast of the Mediterranean Sea, at the western edge of Israel.*

So where did Israel get its name? Israel was named after Abraham's grandson, Jacob, whom God later renamed "Israel."

Jacob got this new name after an all-night wrestling match with an opponent whom Jacob comes to believe is God Himself. At the end of the struggle, Jacob's opponent declares, "Your name will no

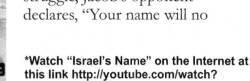

*Watch "Israel's Name" on the Internet at this link http://youtube.com/watch?v=1BgR7qBf_Zk

Facing page: One of the guides at the Genesis Land holds a camel for riders to mount. Above: Another guide shows the route Abraham took from Ur to Israel, before the guide gave us a camel ride of our own.

longer be Jacob, but Israel, because you have struggled with God and with men and have overcome" (Genesis 32:28). "Israel" means struggles, or strives, with God.

So the land of Israel was named after the man who lived there. His twelve sons and their families became the twelve "tribes" of Israel and spread out to live throughout the land. The Bible says that the borders of Israel at that time extended from the desert in the south to Lebanon in the north, and from the Euphrates River on the east to the western sea, or Mediterranean, on the west (see Deuteronomy 11:24 and Joshua 3:1-4).

The land of Israel was actually promised to Jacob's grandfather, Abraham, years earlier, which is why the land of Israel is often referred to as the "promised land."

What I love about reading these passages in the Bible is that they are continual reminders to me that God keeps His promises, whether they are to all of humanity, as in the case of God's promise to Noah that God would never again destroy the earth with a flood, or to a particular nation, as in this case of God's promise to the Israelites that He would bring them into this land, and then bring them back again if they were ever taken away. When God makes a promise, He keeps it!

Here's the original promise that God made to Abraham way back in the twelfth chapter of the Bible, about 4,000 years ago. God said to Abraham:

"Leave your country, your people and your father's household and go to the land I will show you. I will make you into a great nation and I will bless you; I will make your name great, and you will be a blessing. I will bless those who bless

Left and Below: A modern day performer recreates the role of Eliezer, one of Abraham's servants, and invites us in to a feast at "Abraham's Tent."

you, and whoever curses you I will curse; and all peoples on earth will be blessed through you" (Genesis 12:1-3).

So Abraham obeyed and went. And when Abraham got there, God gave him this promise:

"Lift up your eyes from where you are and look north and south, east and west. All the land that you see I will give to you and your offspring forever. I will make your offspring like the dust of the earth, so that if anyone could count the dust, then your offspring could be counted. Go, walk through the length and breadth of the land, for I am giving it to you" (Genesis 13:14-17).

God also forewarned Abraham that his descendants one day would be strangers in another country and enslaved for four hundred years, but afterward they would return to the promised land. This took place when a famine came upon Israel, and Israel's sons moved to Egypt to get food. As the sons' families grew in number, they were enslaved by the Egyptians for fear that they would become too powerful.

Four hundred years later, God sent Moses to set the Israelites free and return them to their homeland. God reminded the Israelites of His promise, saying to them as they approached the promised land:

Above: A river flows through the beautiful hills in Dan at the northernmost edge of Israel.

"Every place where you set your foot will be yours: Your territory will extend from the desert to Lebanon, and from the Euphrates River to the western sea" (Deuteronomy 11:24, and again in Joshua 1:3-4).

Almost a thousand years later, the Israelites were taken captive again, this time to Babylon. But again, God promised that one day they would return to their land. God told the prophet

Above: A camel ride at the Genesis Land brings the Bible to life, recalling Abraham's pilgrimage across these same mountains over 4,000 years ago.

Jeremiah to buy a field in Israel, even though they were about to be taken away, to let the people know that one day they would return again and that,

"Houses, fields and vineyards will again be bought in this land." (Jeremiah 32:15).

They did return about seventy years later. Another five hundred or so years later, Jesus was born in Israel. Except for a few years when Jesus was young, when his parents took Him to Egypt to protect Him from King Herod, Jesus spent His entire life and ministry in the land of Israel.

And when Jesus comes back again, He'll return to the land of His birth, to Israel.

God keeps His promises!

From Genesis to Revelation, God talks about His promises regarding both the land and the people of Israel. It is a land that is truly precious to God. The Bible says,

"It is a land the LORD your God cares for; the eyes of the LORD your God are continually on it from the beginning of the year to its end" (Deuteronomy 11:12).

And it's a land that reminds us that God keeps His promises, whether they're made to all of humanity, or to particular nations, or to individual people like you and like me.

God loves you, He cares about your life, and He wants to see you accomplish all that He has prepared in advance for you to do. If God has made you a promise, hold onto it! God keeps His promises.

Let's pray:

Father, thank You for the promises that You have made throughout history, and the promises that You have made to us in our lifetime. Lord, help us to remember Your promises, and to hold onto them tightly, knowing that You will always keep them. In Jesus' name, Amen.

Below and right: Abraham was called to go to the vast expanse of land that later took the name of his grandson, whom God renamed from Jacob to Israel.

Lesson 2

WHAT HAPPENED IN CAESAREA?

Today we're headed up the coast of the Mediterranean Sea to the city of Caesarea. Why Caesarea? Because something remarkable happened there about 2,000 years ago. To see what happened, take a look at the short video clip at the link to the right, then read on to see how this story can apply to your life today.*

So what happened in Caesarea? This is where Peter preached the good news about Jesus to Cornelius. And what makes it so remarkable? Because this is where God made it crystal clear that Jesus didn't come just as a Savior for the Jews, but for *anyone* who would believe in Him.

The other thing that's remarkable about this story is the way God spoke to Peter and Cornelius. God spoke in a way that was very specific, helping each of them know exactly what God wanted them to do next in their lives. Wouldn't all of us love to have God do that for us!

The truth is, He can, and often does, and if we read the story carefully, we can see some clues as to why God spoke to these two so clearly.

*Watch "Caesarea" on the Internet at this link http://youtube.com/watch? v=F97frToCVYo

Facing page: An auditorium at Caesarea from the time of King Herod has been renovated and is still in use today. Above: The ancient aqueducts of Caesarea.

Above: Our group stops to read the biblical account of Paul's imprisonment in Caesarea, on the very spot where the prison would have stood within the palace complex.

Here's how God spoke to Cornelius:

At Caesarea there was a man named Cornelius, a centurion in what was known as the Italian Regiment. He and all his family were devout and God-fearing; he gave generously to those in need and prayed to God regularly. One day at about three in the afternoon he had a vision. He distinctly saw an angel of God, who came to him and said, "Cornelius!"

Cornelius stared at him in fear. "What is it, Lord?" he asked.

The angel answered, "Your prayers and gifts to the poor have come up as a memorial offering

before God. Now send men to Joppa to bring back a man named Simon who is called Peter. He is staying with Simon the tanner, whose house is by the sea" (Acts 10:1-6).

And here's how God spoke to Peter:

About noon the following day as they were on their journey and approaching the city, Peter went up on the roof to pray. He became hungry and wanted something to eat, and while the meal was being prepared, he fell into a trance. He saw heaven opened and something like a large sheet being let down to earth by its four corners. It contained all kinds of four-footed animals, as well as reptiles of the earth and birds of the air. Then a voice told him, "Get up, Peter. Kill and eat."

"Surely not, Lord!" Peter replied. "I have never eaten anything impure or unclean."

The voice spoke to him a second time, "Do not call anything impure that God has made clean."

This happened three times, and immediately the sheet was taken back to heaven.

While Peter was wondering about the meaning of the vision, the men sent by Cornelius found out where Simon's house was and stopped at the gate. They called out, asking if Simon who was known as Peter was staying there.

While Peter was still thinking about the vision, the Spirit said to him, "Simon, three men are looking for you. So get up and go downstairs. Do not hesitate to go with them, for I have sent them" (Acts 10:9-20).

Did you catch why God spoke the way He did to Cornelius? And why God might have spoken to Peter the way He did?

In Cornelius' case, the Bible says, "He [Cornelius] and all his family were devout and God-fearing; he gave generously to those in need and prayed to God regularly." The angel then says very specifically: "Your prayers and gifts to the poor have come up as a memorial offering before God." Then the angel proceeds to share with him what to do next.

And as for Peter's case, his story begins with the words, "Peter went up on the roof to pray." It was during that time of prayer that God spoke to Peter and revealed to him what he needed to do next, too.

Prayer in its most basic form is having a conversation with God. Sometimes it

Below: The ruins of a 10,000 seat hippodrome have been recently unearthed along the coast, as coastal waters have receded in recent years, exposing the previous coastline. This corner contained the most prized seats, as chariots would have careened out of control when taking this curve at high speeds.

Left and Above: The house of Simon the Tanner still stands along the coast in Joppa, at the end of the street pictured above, and is still a private residence today. Below: Cats play in Joppa.

may feel like it's only a one-way conversation, but I've found that the more I pray, and the more that I wait for and listen for and expect Him to answer, the more I actually hear God speak to me in return! It's not rocket-science, but it does take is faith. And in Cornelius' example, he didn't rely on his faith alone, but he was continually demonstrating his faith in God by his good deeds. He was putting his money where his mouth was, so to speak. Or, as Jesus said it: "For where your treasure is, there your heart will be also" (Matthew 6:22).

The beauty of this story is that God was not only moved by the prayers and gifts of these men, but God answered their prayers in a way that went beyond either of their expectations. For Cornelius, it opened up a whole new understanding of who God was and what

He could do next to come into a more full and right relationship with Him. And for Peter, this opened a whole new door of ministry that he would have never realized even needed to be opened without his prayers and God's response, that God wanted him to proclaim the good news about Jesus even to the Gentiles, meaning anyone who was not Jewish.

These are great lessons for any of us who want to experience more of God in our lives, and for anyone who wants to serve Him more fully.

If you've already put your faith in Christ, today's a good day to thank God for what happened in Caesarea! And if you've never put your faith in Christ, today's a good day to do that, too! Let God's Spirit fall upon you as it fell upon all who heard Peter's message that day when he said:

"All the prophets testify about Him [Jesus] that everyone who believes in Him receives forgiveness of sins through His name" (Acts 10:34-36,43).

Let's pray:

Father, thank You for speaking to people so specifically about events that were about to change their lives so dramatically. We pray that You would speak to us again today, so that we may hear from You and do all that is on Your heart for us to do. In Jesus' name, Amen.

Below: A Roman aqueduct stretches on and on, and once brought fresh water down from the hills to the coastal town of Caesarea.

Lesson 3

WHAT HAPPENED ON MOUNT CARMEL?

As we continue our devotional tour of the Holy Land, we're heading further north along the Mediterranean coast, this time to the top of Mount Carmel. It's a beautiful spot where a powerful story took place about 3,000 years ago.

To hear a summary of the story in under two minutes, including how it applies to your life today, click the link to the video at the right.* Then continue reading the rest of the message below that to learn how God can answer your prayers in

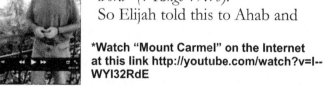

extraordinary ways, even though you may feel like just an "ordinary person."

So what happened on Mount Carmel? That's where Elijah challenged the prophets of Baal and Asherah to a dramatic showdown. Many of the Israelites had strayed from God, worshiping Baal and Asherah instead. The situation had gotten so bad that God told Elijah to go to the Israelite king, Ahab, and tell him:

"...there will be neither dew nor rain in the next few years except at my word" (1 Kings 17:1b).

So Elijah told this to Ahab and

*Watch "Mount Carmel" on the Internet at this link http://youtube.com/watch?v=I--WYI32RdE

Facing page: Elijah's victory at Mount Carmel led to the death Ahab and his wife, Jezebel. Above: A frieze depicts Elijah's showdown with Ahab's prophets, and a bench made of rocks sits in the garden.

Above: The view from Mount Carmel extends in all directions, as shown by this painting at the top of the mountain, pointing to cities throughout Israel.

the rain stopped. All of Israel began to suffer. But neither Ahab nor the people turned back to God. After three and a half years, God told Elijah to go back to Ahab and tell him that the rain was about to come again.

Elijah went to Ahab and told him to meet him on Mount Carmel, where the dramatic showdown took place, and where God would answer Elijah's prayers in a way that convinced the Israelites to turn their hearts back to God. It was after this that Elijah climbed to the top of Mount Carmel, bent down to the ground to pray, and by the end of the day, the rain poured down.

It's one of the coolest stories in the Old Testament, and if you haven't read it yet, or haven't read it in awhile, I'd like to encourage you to read the whole thing sometime this week. You'll find it in the book of 1 Kings, chapters 17-19.

While there are tons of helpful and encouraging lessons from these chapters —ranging from how God can provide for your needs even during a famine to how God can give you the courage you need to do some very difficult things—the lesson I'd like to focus on today deals with the question of why God sometimes answers your prayers and other times doesn't—or at least not in the way you expected.

Sometimes God can knock your socks off with His answers to your prayers, like He did with Elijah's prayers on Mount Carmel. The book of James even holds up Elijah's story as an example of just how powerful prayer can be. James says:

"The prayer of a righteous man is powerful and effective. Elijah was a man just like us. He prayed earnestly that it would not rain, and it did not rain on the land for three and a half years. Again he prayed, and the heavens gave rain, and the earth produced its crops" (James 5:16b-18).

So Elijah was human, just like us, and God heard and answered his prayers in a powerful way. Yet did you know that not long after this event, Elijah prayed another prayer—one that he seems to

Below: The view down one side of Mount Carmel extends to the Valley of Jezreel in the distance.

Above: A curious cat watches those who make the trip to the top of Mount Carmel.

have prayed as earnestly as the one before —yet God didn't do what Elijah asked?

This other prayer took place after the showdown at Mount Carmel, when Elijah had to run for his life because Ahab's wife had vowed to hunt Elijah down until he was dead. So Elijah ran as far as he could until he he was thoroughly exhausted. The Bible says,

"He came to a broom tree, sat down under it and prayed that he might die. 'I have had enough, Lord. Take my life; I am no better than my ancestors'" (1 Kings 19:4b).

Then he lay down under the tree and fell asleep.

But God didn't answer this prayer, at least in the way that Elijah wanted Him to answer it. God didn't take his life. God wanted Elijah to live, for God still had more for Elijah to do with his life.

So God sent Elijah an angel. The angel woke him up and gave him something warm to eat. After eating two of these angel-cooked meals, Elijah gained enough strength to travel another forty days and forty nights until he reached Horeb, the mountain of God. And it was there on Mount Horeb that God Himself appeared to Elijah in a very personal way,

"...*in a gentle whisper*" *(1 Kings 19:12b).*

God didn't give Elijah what he wanted, but He gave him something much better: an angel of encouragement, strength for the journey, and a one-on-one visit with Elijah himself.

I want to encourage you today that God can answer your prayers as dramatically and powerfully as He answered Elijah's prayers for rain. But God can also answer your prayers like He answered Elijah's second prayer, not necessarily giving you what you want or expect, but giving you something truly better.

God loves you. He cares about your life. And He has things that He truly wants to do in and through your life. Keep praying earnestly that God's will would be done here on earth, through you, just as God's will was done through Elijah's prayers at Mount Carmel.

Let's pray:

Above: A garden at the top of Mount Carmel features a variety of plant life and rock formations, and serves as a beautiful setting for considering the faithfulness of God.

Father, thank You for Elijah's example of what it means to pray earnestly for Your will to be done. Give us Your wisdom and insight into the situations in our lives today so that we can pray for Your will to be done in them as well. We love You and thank You for hearing our prayers. In Jesus' name, Amen.

Lesson 4

WHAT'S GOING TO HAPPEN AT MEGIDDO?

You may have never heard of Megiddo before, but it's more than likely you've heard about what is going to happen there one day. And with a little help from the Hebrew language, you may realize that you have heard of Megiddo before in just a slightly different form. Take a look at the short video at the link to the right to see this historical place with an important future.* Then keep reading below to see how it can affect your life today.

So what's going to happen at

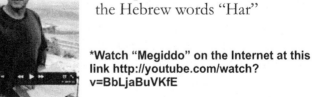

Megiddo? That's where Christ will return for the final battle of all the nations of the world.

The book of Revelation prophecies about this coming battle, saying that the spirits of demons will go out to the kings of the whole world:

"...to gather them for the battle on the great day of God Almighty. ... Then they gathered the kings together to the place that in Hebrew is called Armageddon" (Revelation 16:14b, 16).

Armageddon comes to us from the Hebrew words "Har"

*Watch "Megiddo" on the Internet at this link http://youtube.com/watch?v=BbLjaBuVKfE

Facing page: The final battle of the world will take place on the plains of Megiddo. Above: Megiddo was also once the site of King Solomon's stables, the remains of which can still be explored today.

Above: Even an ordinary bus ride seems to exude a special aura for those traveling through the plains of Megiddo!

has been depicted in so many apocalyptic books and movies. But perhaps more sobering to me is the fact that since God has fulfilled so many prophecies found in the Bible already, it just follows reason that He will one day fulfill the rest as well, including the prophecies about this cataclysmic battle.

And from history, we know that this location has served as a battlefield for many battles before. King Josiah died here about 600 years before Christ in a battle with Pharaoh Neco of Egypt (2 Kings 23:29) and Sir Edmund Allenby of Britain launched a massive attack here during the first World War, to name a few. The role of Megiddo as a military battlefield was summed up by Napoleon, one of the foremost military leaders of all time when he saw Megiddo in the early 1800's. He is quoted as saying: *"All the armies of the world could maneuver their forces on this vast plain ... There is no place in the whole world more suited for war than this ... It is the most natural battleground on the whole earth." (The Battles of Armageddon, pg. 142).*

meaning hill, and Megiddo, referring to the city found there. So Har Megiddo means the hill of Megiddo, which translates for us into "Armageddon."

It's an unusual sight to look out and see the cars and trucks and buses going back and forth about their business at the base of the hill, knowing that one day all the nations of the world will gather here for that final epic battle, the one which

And Megiddo is situated in a primary trade route at the north of Israel, a location from which you can see the hills of neighboring countries who are even now poised and ready to do battle here. The inspiring thing about standing on the hill of Megiddo is that it makes me want to do right before God and men.

While God is certainly more forgiving and patient than I or anyone else I know has ever been or would ever be, there is still a limit to His patience. At some point, He must deal with sin, or He wouldn't be a very good judge at all.

As much as I'd rather not think about it, there comes a time when justice must be done and we will all have to face judgment for what we've done. This day is often referred to in the Bible as the "Day of the Lord." It's a day that is referred to over twenty-five times in the Bible, including both the Old and New Testaments.

Several weeks before writing this message I had a dream in which I got an invitation in the mail. It was an invitation to an "end of the world party" to be held on June 6-7, just a few weeks from then. I don't put much stock in the dream as anything prophetic, as even Jesus Himself said that no one knows the day or hour when these things will happen, but only the Father (Matthew 24:36). But the dream did help me to think a little more clearly that day when I woke up!

I wondered: What would I do differently if I knew that the world was really going to end in just a few weeks? How would I spend my time? Who do I still need to talk to and what would I say? How can I help more people come into a relationship with Christ so that when the final battle does come they're on the winning side?

Below and right: There's something surreal about looking at sites with prophetic significance, set against the backdrop of present-day life.

31

Left and above: Megiddo is still being excavated, uncovering layers and layers of civilizations that have occupied this spot.

call and what would you say? And why are you waiting?" God wants more than anything else to have a relationship with each one of us, including you and those around you. He knows how sin affects our lives in ways that we could never even understand. And He wants us to be freed from those sins.

That's why He sent Jesus to earth, to die for our sins, so that all who put their faith in Him will be forgiven of their sins and spend eternity with Him in heaven.

If you've never put your faith in Christ, I encourage you to do it today. Don't wait any longer, for no one knows the day or hour when He will return. And if you've already put your faith in Christ, share that faith with someone today.

Give them a call. Write them a letter. Send them a text, an email, or a link to this video and devotional. Remind them that:

And today I wonder: How would it affect your life if you knew that the end were just a few weeks away? It reminds me of a quote from Stephen Levine:

"If you were going to die soon and had only one phone call you could make, who would you

"The Lord is not slow in keeping His promise, as some understand slowness. He is patient with you, not wanting anyone to perish, but everyone to come to repentance." (2 Peter 3:9).

Let's pray:

Father, thank You for fulfilling so many of the prophecies of the Bible already and we trust that You will fulfill the rest in due time. Lord, help us to live our lives in such a way that they become shining testimonies to You and help us to encourage those around us to put their faith in Christ so they can be on the winning side in the final battle as well. In Jesus' name, Amen.

Above right: A pomegranate dangles on a tree at Megiddo. Below: The valley which Napoleon described as "the most natural battleground on the whole earth."

Lesson 5

WHAT HAPPENED IN NAZARETH?

Our next stop on this devotional tour of the Holy Land is a city that wasn't known as one of the hot spots of Israel. In fact, the Bible quotes Nathanael as saying,

"Nazareth? Can anything good come from there?" (John 1:46).

But something good did come from there. To hear what happened there, take a look at this short video that I shot while at the Nazareth Village in Israel, a re-creation of what the city might have looked like back in Jesus'

day.* Then read on below to find out how God can work in your life through even the most difficult situations to accomplish His plans.

So what happened in Nazareth? This is where Jesus grew up. It was also the hometown of Mary and Joseph and the place where the angel Gabriel came to Mary and said:

"Do not be afraid, Mary, you have found favor with God. You will be with child and give birth to a son, and you are to give Him the name Jesus" (Luke 1:30-31).

*Watch "Nazareth" on the Internet at this link http://youtube.com/watch?v=zC6f8FTHdOA

Facing page: A swing hangs from a tree at the Nazareth Village, a re-creation of Nazareth at the time of Christ. Above: The Nazareth YMCA's mission is that youth will grow like Christ, as noted in Luke 2:52.

But Jesus wasn't born in Nazareth. In fact, His route to ending up here seemed rather circuitous.

Because of the Roman census, Mary and Joseph had to return to Bethlehem at the time of Jesus' birth. Then after Jesus' birth, Herod found out that a new "King of the Jews" may have been born in Bethlehem and began a killing spree of all the newborn boys there, so Mary and Joseph fled to Egypt. After Herod died, Mary and Joseph returned again to Israel and went back to their hometown of Nazareth.

It may have seemed like Jesus and his parents were being yanked around by governments and kings, making their lives difficult at critical times. I try to imagine Mary being nine months pregnant, having to ride on a donkey to Bethlehem, then finding no place to stay and give birth to her child. I try to imagine their having to flee that city because a crazed king wanted to kill their young Son. I try to imagine their having to move to a foreign country when Jesus was small, with all the changes such a move from family and friends must have entailed.

Yet I'm encouraged to think that each stop along the way was not random. Each move was part of God's divine plan for both Jesus and His parents. Hundreds of years earlier each stop along the way had already been foretold.

Getting to Bethlehem was the first

Left: Tools of the trade in the days of Jesus: a mule pulls a millstone in circles so its massive weight can crush the olives beneath it, pressing the oil out.

stop in fulfilling the prophecies concerning the Messiah. When the chief priests and teachers of the law were asked where the Messiah was to be born, they replied:

"In Bethlehem in Judea, for this is what the prophet has written: 'But you, Bethlehem, in the land of Judah, are by no means least among the rulers of Judah; for out of you will come a ruler who will be the shepherd of my people Israel' " *(Matthew 2:5-6).*

The trip to Egypt fulfilled the next stop. As Matthew said:

"And so was fulfilled what the Lord had said through the prophet: 'Out of Egypt I called my son' " *(Matthew 2:15).*

And the return to Nazareth fulfilled the third stop. As Matthew said about His return:

"So was fulfilled what was said through the prophets: 'He will be called a Nazarene'" *(Matthew 2:23).*

So rather than a seemingly random

chain of events moving Jesus from place to place, God had a plan and a way to use all of those events to bring about His will.

How does all this relate to you and me? I take encouragement from the fact that even when it looks like our lives are being pushed and pulled in various

Above: More tools of the trade: a plow that hooks onto an ox, and a drill made of a piece of wood and a metal bit, spun in circles by a string on a stick. Below: Another cat relaxes on the steps of the Nazareth YMCA.

Left: A recreation of the synagogue in Nazareth, where Jesus read from the scroll of Isaiah. Above: A flame in an oil filled lamp, made in Nazareth, reminds us to share the light of Christ with the world.

directions by people, governments, or difficult situations, that it may actually be God doing the pushing and pulling to fulfill His plans for our lives! And if it's not God doing the actual pushing and pulling, at least it's no surprise to Him what we're going through. If God was able to foretell and use all of the events and situations that would surround the birth and life of His Son, then He is able to foretell and use all of the events and situations that we'll face in our lives as well.

Rather than being upset at others who sometimes seem to be in control of our lives—whether it's a boss or a job, a government official or a family member, a friend or an enemy—we can trust that

God is the one who controls them all. And even if He doesn't control them directly, for He has given each of us free will as well, God does know the hearts of men and women and He can work all things together for good.

Although Nazareth wasn't a hot spot in the Holy Land in Jesus' day, God wasn't bothered by its reputation. It was here where God chose to raise His Son and it was here where the Bible says,

"Jesus grew in wisdom and stature, and in favor with God and men" (Luke 2:52).

Your life is not random and the places where you live and work and eat and sleep are not arbitrary, regardless of the reputation they may or may not have. God has a plan for you, for your life, and for the situations that you're facing even right now. He wants you to trust Him fully with that plan and follow Him wherever He leads—whether that's staying where He wants you to stay or going where He wants you to go.

Trust Him with every aspect of your life and let Him take control of the direction it takes. It's good to make plans for our lives, but it's also good to let God take control of those plans when He has a better one. As it says in the book of Proverbs:

"In his heart a man plans his course, but the LORD determines his steps" (Proverbs 16:9).

Let's pray:

Father, thank You for taking the random events of our lives and giving them purpose and meaning in ways that go beyond what we could think or imagine. Lord, we commit to trusting You again today, giving You full control over the course of our lives. In Jesus' name, Amen.

Below: The city of Nazareth today.

Lesson 6

What Happened On The Sea Of Galilee?

Today, we're visiting the Sea of Galilee. If you'd like to see—and hear—what the water looks like at the Sea of Galilee today, take a look at the short video at the link at the right.* It's a beautiful spot in the land of Israel and the site of some of Jesus' most memorable miracles. Then read on to see how putting your faith in Christ can help you through some of the toughest situations in your life.

So what happened on the Sea of Galilee? This is where Jesus spent much of His time after He left His boyhood home of Nazareth. In the coming weeks, I'll be talking about several of the miracles that took place here that touched people's hearts and lives.

But today I'd like to focus on two that took place out on the sea itself: when Jesus walked on water and when He calmed the storm that threatened the lives of His disciples.

Jesus is an expert at walking through storms. The miracle that He did on the Sea of Galilee wasn't the first time He displayed

*Watch "Sea of Galilee" on the Internet at this link http://youtube.com/watch?v=ygH1gV7LT74

Facing page: You can still take a boat ride on the Sea of Galilee, which measures 8 miles wide by 13 miles long. Above: The coastline of the Sea of Galilee, and a time of worship on the water.

Above and left: Shells line the shore along the Sea of Galilee, attesting to the wide array of life that lives within its fresh waters.

His giftedness for this. Just before coming to the Sea of Galilee, Jesus walked unscathed through another storm that threatened to take His own life.

Maybe you remember that when Jesus lived in Nazareth, He went to the synagogue one day and read from the scroll of Isaiah. At first, all the people spoke well of Him, being amazed at "the gracious words that came from His lips." But after quoting from the words of Isaiah—referring to the Messiah that was to come—Jesus added:

"Today this scripture is fulfilled in your hearing" (Luke 4:21b).

Imagine growing up in the same city with Jesus—the guy down the block who did carpentry with His dad—then He gets up and says that He's the Messiah, the One about whom the prophet Isaiah had written about some 700 years earlier. You'd think that Jesus was either a lunatic or a liar. He couldn't possibly be telling the truth, could He?

So the crowd turned on Him. The Bible says:

"All the people in the synagogue were furious when they heard this. They got up, drove Him out of the town, and took Him to the brow of the hill on which the town was built, in order to throw Him down the cliff. But He walked right through the crowd and went on His way" (Luke 4:28-30).

The crowd went from calm to stormy in a matter of seconds. They went from praising Jesus to taking Him to the edge of a cliff to throw Him off within a matter of minutes. But Jesus wasn't phased by their words of praise nor their acts of violence. He simply said what He had to say, then "walked right through the crowd and went on His way."

So when the storm came up on His disciples on the Sea of Galilee some time later, Jesus wasn't phased by it either. He and His disciples had just finished a long day of ministering to thousands, having heard earlier in the day that John the Baptist had just been beheaded. Jesus headed off to a mountainside to pray, telling His disciples to get into the boat and head to the other side.

The story picks up here:

When evening came, He was there alone, but the boat was already a considerable distance from land, buffeted by the waves because the wind was against it.

During the fourth watch of the night Jesus went out to them, walking on the lake. When the disciples saw Him walking on the lake, they were terrified. "It's a ghost," they said, and cried out in fear.

But Jesus immediately

said to them: "Take courage! It is I. Don't be afraid."

That's when Jesus famously called Peter to come out to Him and walk on the water and which Peter did until he saw the wind and the waves and started to sink again. So Jesus reached out His hand and took hold of Peter's and pulled him back up.

The story finishes by saying:

And when they climbed into the boat, the wind died down. Then those who were in the

Right: The "Jesus Boat" is a fishing boat from the time of Christ that was found in the mud at the bottom of the Sea of Galilee during a recent drought—having been unusually preserved for so long by not being exposed to air for all these years.

boat worshiped Him, saying, "Truly You are the Son of God" (Matthew 14:23b-33).

There are two things that I'd like to mention about this storm. The first is that Jesus is the one who sent them into it. And the second is that Jesus is the one who brought them out of it.

Above and below: A restful day on the Sea of Galilee, and a beautiful hotel hotel by the Sea at night.

Just like in Nazareth, Jesus didn't worry about the wind and the waves. In the case of the angry crowd, Jesus had nothing to fear. It was the crowd who was fearful by what Jesus was saying and acted wrongfully because of it. Jesus did what was right and when He was done He simply walked through the crowd and went on His way.

In the same way, when Jesus needed to get to the other side of the lake, He wasn't phased by the fact that strong waves lay ahead. He sent His disciples into the waves and He went into them Himself afterward. Jesus wasn't afraid of the storm. Jesus just kept doing what He needed to do and His disciples did what He told them to. There are times when I've felt like I was being thrown into a storm—and it seemed like it was Jesus who was throwing me into it! I've learned that the best thing to do in those times is to hold onto Jesus as tight as I can. I know that Jesus knows best how to walk through them, whether I'm facing an angry crowd or some wind and some waves.

Above and below: The Sea of Galilee is an ever-present reminder that God is the One who can give us peace in the midst of our storms.

You may find yourself in the middle of a storm right now, too. The circumstances of your life may be buffeting against you. You may be facing things that are threatening your health, your family, your relationships, your job, your career, your finances or your friends. The threats may be very real and the prospects ahead may look very grim.

I want to encourage you to hold onto Jesus as tight as you can. Keep walking through the wind and the waves.

Keep walking towards Jesus, the Messiah, the Author and Sustainer of your life. And even if you start to sink, know that Jesus is right beside you to take hold of your hands and pull you in close. Hold on tight and never let Him go. He's the One who knows best how to walk through a storm. Let Him speak to you the words He spoke to His disciples that night on the Sea of Galilee:

"Take courage, it is I! Don't be afraid."

Let's pray:

Father, thank You for sending Jesus to help us through the storms we face. Thank You for reminding us that it's sometimes even Jesus who sends us into the storms in the first place. Lord, help us to have the faith to trust in Him, no matter what, and to trust that whether it's Him who sent us into the storm or not, that He's the One who can bring us through it. In Jesus' name, Amen.

Lesson 7

WHAT HAPPENED
IN CAPERNAUM?

I was surprised
when I visited the city
of Capernaum to learn about
all the things that Jesus did
there. It shouldn't have been surprising,
however, for Capernaum served as the
home base for most of Jesus'
ministry, having moved there
when He left His boyhood home
of Nazareth. To hear about some
of the things that Jesus did in
Capernaum, take a look at this
forty-second video. Then read on
to see how Jesus is still working
today in the same ways that He

did in Capernaum.*

So what happened in Capernaum?
This is where Jesus healed many people.
Here's a sampling of the healings that
took place there:
* *He healed the centurion's servant*
* *He healed the paralytic and forgave him of his sins*
* *He healed the woman who had been bleeding for twelve years*
* *He healed Jairus' daughter, raising her from the dead*
* *and He healed two blind men.*

The common thread running

*Watch "Capernaum" on the Internet at this link http://youtube.com/watch?v=9eIvdP-nLrE

Facing page and above: The synagogue in Capernaum still stands today, the site of many of Jesus' teachings and healings, and located in the town that Jesus called home during his ministry years.

Above and right: Peter's house was in Capernaum, the site where Jesus healed Peter's mother-in-law, and also the site where the early Christians are said to have met together.

through each of these stories is that the people were healed by faith in Christ.

In the story of the centurion's servant, Jesus commends his faith, saying:

"I tell you the truth, I have not found anyone in Israel with such great faith..." Then Jesus said to the centurion, "Go! It will be done just as you believed it would." And his servant was healed at that very hour (Matthew 8:10b, 13).

In the story of the paralytic, Jesus took note of his friends' faith:

When Jesus saw their faith, He said to the paralytic,

"Take heart, son; your sins are forgiven." ... Then He said to the paralytic, "Get up, take your mat and go home." And the man got up and went home. (Matthew 9:2b,6b-7).

In the story of the woman who had been bleeding for twelve years, Jesus said:

"Take heart, daughter, your faith has healed you." And the woman was healed from that moment (Matthew 9:22b).

In the story of Jairus' daughter, Jesus said:

"Don't be afraid; just believe." ... He took her by the hand and said to her, 'Talitha koum!' (which means, 'Little girl, I say to you, get up!'). Immediately the girl stood up and walked around... (Mark 5:36b, 41-42a).

And in the story of the two blind men, before Jesus healed them, He asked them a question:

"Do you believe that I am able to do this?"
"Yes, Lord," they replied.
Then He touched their eyes and said, "According to your faith will it be done to you";

Right and below: A unique church now sits—lifted up off the ground —above Peter's house. Visitors can still see the house below through special glass that has been suspended over it.

and their sight was restored (Matthew 9:28b-30a).

It was this last story that surprised me the most when I read that it took place in Capernaum, for it was this story that inspired me to put my faith in Christ 23 years ago. I had no idea that it took place there in Capernaum until I was preparing for this trip to Israel. It was a detail I had overlooked at the time.

When I had read the story 23 years ago, I was walking along a road in Houston, Texas. I was about 7,000 miles away from Capernaum and it was about 2,000 years later. I was asking God for a healing in my own life. I felt like Jesus was asking me the same question: "Eric, do you believe I am able to do this, too?"

I thought about everything Jesus had ever done—how He healed the sick, walked on water and raised the dead. I thought if anyone could do it, Jesus could. So I put my hand up in the air, and for the first time in my life, I truly put my faith in Christ. Like the blind men, I said, "Yes, Lord." And like the

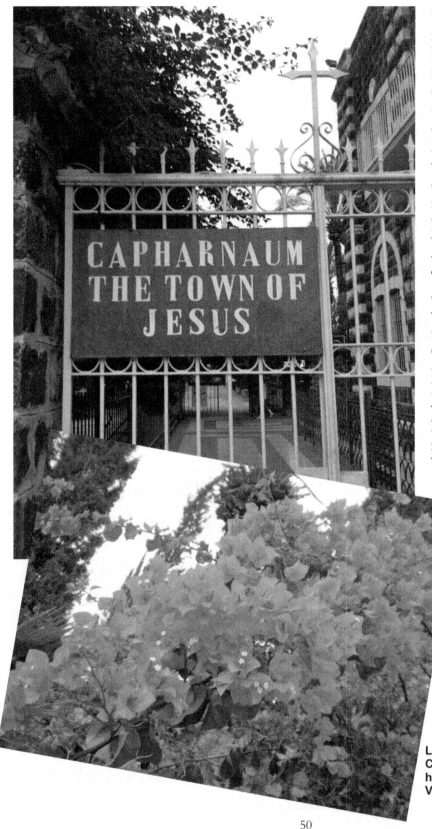

blind men, I was healed in that moment.

By the next day I had put my faith in Christ for everything in my life. I asked Him to forgive me of my sins and trusted Him to take me to live with Him forever when I died. (If you'd like to read more of this story, you can read it on my website at www.theranch.org.) The course of my life changed that day, and it was all based on a story that took place in Capernaum. To stand there when we visited Israel and think about what happened then and how it had affected me now was astounding. What a blessing that these stories have been recorded for us and can touch our lives in such life-changing ways. Faith in Christ is a powerful thing. But you don't have to take my word for it —you can take His word for it! According to His word, it was by faith that the

Left: The name Capernaum, or Capharnaum as it is spelled here, means "Nahum's Village."

50

centurion's servant was healed; by faith, the paralytic was forgiven of his sins and healed of his paralysis; by faith, the woman who had been bleeding for twelve years was healed; by faith, Jairus' daughter was raised from the dead; and by faith, the sight of the blind men had restored.

If you need God to do something in your life that you can't seem to do on your own, I'd like to encourage you to put your faith in Christ, and keep putting your faith in Him for everything in Your life. You'll be glad you did.

Let's pray:

Father, thank You for the inspiring stories of faith that took place in Capernaum. I pray that You would reach out to us in the same way today, doing the impossible for those who are willing to put their faith in You. In Jesus' name, Amen.

Right: More cats! This one resting in the beautiful gardens where Jesus lived during His ministry years.

Lesson 8

WHAT HAPPENED ON THE MOUNT OF BEATITUDES?

The Mount of Beatitudes is one of the many hills that rise up around the Sea of Galilee. It was here that Jesus preached His famous "Sermon on the Mount," blessing thousands of people who had gathered to hear Him speak. But why is it called the Mount of "Beatitudes," and what else did Jesus do on this hill for those who gathered here? Take a look at the short video at the link at the right to hear more and to get a view of the mountain itself.* Then read on to see how Jesus can bless you today—and how you can be a blessing to Him!

So what happened on the Mount of Beatitudes? "Beatitude" means "blessing," and this is where Jesus spoke about the many blessings that God offers to those who believe in Him, such as:

"Blessed are the poor in spirit, for theirs is the kingdom of heaven. Blessed are those who mourn, for they will be comforted. Blessed are the meek, for they will inherit the earth. Blessed are those who hunger and thirst for righteousness, for they will be filled..." (Matthew 5:3-6).

*Watch "Mount of Beatitudes" on the Internet at this link http://youtube.com/watch?v=ZVe4XRKOWsc

Facing page and above: The Mount of Beatitudes on the hillside along the Sea of Galilee, where Jesus spoke His famous "beatitudes," or blessings, and where thousands gathered to hear Him speak.

Left and above: The Church of the Beatitudes sits at the top of the hill where Jesus preached, and overlooks the Sea of Galilee.

This is also where Jesus demonstrated His blessings to the crowd by multiplying five loaves of bread and two fish into a feast that fed five thousand. The Bible says:

"Then Jesus directed them to have all the people sit down in groups on the green grass. So they sat down in groups of hundreds and fifties. Taking the five loaves and the two fish and looking up to heaven, He gave thanks and broke the loaves. Then He gave them to His disciples to set before the people. He also divided the two fish among them all. They all ate and were satisfied, and the disciples picked up twelve basketfuls of broken pieces of bread and fish.

The number of the men who had eaten was five thousand" (Mark 6:39-44).

It's a remarkable story, and Jesus still does similar things today. I've written about one such story that happened to me recently on our trip to Israel—and even culminated for me at the very spot where Jesus multiplied the loaves and fishes. (I've included this story at the end of this book, in the concluding chapter called "Making A Chance.")

But as practical as Jesus' teachings are, and as remarkable as His ability to multiply loaves and fish is, Jesus doesn't stop there. He goes a step farther and offers us more: an abundant life in Him. But sometimes we're the ones who shortchange what Jesus has to offer us.

I heard a story about a boy who went to his uncle's farm every summer for a few days. When the boy would arrive, his uncle would greet him with pockets full of nickels jingling at his sides. After a few minutes of talking with each other, the uncle reached into his pocket and handed his nephew a nickel.

Throughout the next few days, the uncle did the same thing over and over, spending a few minutes talking with the boy, then handing him a nickel; doing a chore or two, then handing the boy a nickel; taking a walk down the road together then handing the boy a nickel. By the end of those few days, the uncle's pockets were empty and the boy's pockets were full.

The next summer, the same thing happened. The uncle began with his pockets jangling with nickels and at the end of

their time together, the boy's pockets were full of nickels.

After a few summers, the boy got an idea. The next time he visited his uncle at the farm, he was again greeted by his uncle with his pockets full of nickels. The boy said: "Every summer by the end of my time with you, you always give me all the nickels in your pocket. So I've got an idea. Why don't you just give me all the nickels right now, then I can go do what I want, and you can go do what you want without me around to bother you!"

Below: A cave and a sculpture of Jesus can be seen on the path leading up the hill.

Above: The Mount of Beatitudes serves as a reminder of the many blessings we all have in Christ, whether rich or poor, hungry or well-fed, or filled with joy or grief.

Although the boy's idea had merit at one level, it missed the point entirely at another. The reason the uncle gave the boy the nickels in the first place was because he loved spending as much time with the boy as he could. The uncle wanted to be with his nephew, and their time together always turned out to be precious to them both.

You can almost see this boy's idea start to crop up in the hearts of the people who followed Jesus. The day after Jesus multiplied the loaves and the fishes, more boats arrived at the place where the miracle had occurred, but Jesus was no longer there. The Bible says:

Once the crowd realized that neither Jesus nor His disciples were there, they got into the boats and went to Capernaum in search of Jesus.

When they found Him on the other side of the lake, they asked Him, "Rabbi, when did You get here?"

Jesus answered, "I tell you the truth, you are looking for Me, not because you saw miraculous signs but because you ate the loaves and had your fill. Do not work for food that spoils, but for food that endures to eternal life, which the Son of Man will give you" (John 6:24-27a).

Jesus went on to remind them that God is eager to provide for their daily needs just as He provided bread from heaven—in the form of manna—every day for forty years while the Israelites wandered through the desert. But then Jesus added:

"I am the bread of life. Your forefathers ate the manna in the desert, yet they died. But here is the bread that comes down from heaven, which a man may eat and not die. I am the living bread that came down from heaven. If anyone eats of this bread, he will live forever" (John 6:48-51a).

While Jesus is glad to give you practical advice for living, like He did in the Sermon on the Mount, He wants to give you more. And while He's glad to meet your daily needs, as He did for those who ate the feast on the hillside, He wants to give you more.

Jesus wants to give you a relationship with Him, the living bread that came down from heaven. He doesn't want to just give you money for the trip, He wants to be your companion along the journey. He doesn't want to just give you a roadmap to where you're going, He wants to go with you and guide you there Himself. Your relationship with Jesus takes precedence over everything He could ever teach you, or give you, in a lifetime.

I want to encourage you today: come to Jesus for His teachings, for they can change your life; and come to Him for your daily bread, for

He's still a God who can provide for all your needs with baskets full left over.

But don't stop there. Don't shortchange all that God wants to do for you today. Come to Him for life, and life abundant. Come to Him for a feast that never ends—eternal life with Him, a life that starts here on earth and goes on forever. As Jesus told those on the hillside:

"I am the bread of life. He who comes to Me will never go hungry, and he who believes in Me will never be thirsty....If anyone eats of this bread, he will live forever" (John 6:35,51b).

Let's pray:

Father, thank You for blessing us with Your life and Your words. Help us to look to You for our daily bread, but not to stop there. Help us to look to You for bread that will last forever, bread that comes only through an ongoing relationship with You. In Jesus' name, Amen.

Right: Sunset, as seen from the Mount of Beatitudes.

Lesson 9

WHAT HAPPENED AT CAESAREA PHILIPPI?

Caesarea Philippi is on the northern edge of Israel in a beautiful region known as Dan. But the things that took place there weren't always so beautiful. To find out more, watch the short video at the link at the right, then read on to find out how God can do beautiful things for you even if you're in a very dark place.*

So what happened at Caesarea Philippi? This is where God revealed to Peter that Jesus was the Christ, the Son of the living God.

Caesarea Philippi was also home to a cultic temple carved into the side of a massive rock that was called at that time "the gates of hell." It was so named because of the infant sacrifices that took place there in the years leading up to the time of Christ.

With this background in mind, the words that Jesus spoke on this spot are even more meaningful. Here's what happened, as recorded in the book of Matthew:

When Jesus came to the region of Caesarea Philippi, He asked His disciples, "Who do people say the Son

*Watch "Caesarea Philippi" on the Internet at this link http://youtube.com/watch?v=hhvJnF8bPgl

Facing page and above: The Temple of Pan, the site of many pagan, child sacrifices, is also the site where God revealed to Peter that Jesus was "the Christ, the Son of the Living God."

of Man is?"

They replied, "Some say John the Baptist; others say Elijah; and still others, Jeremiah or one of the prophets."

"But what about you?" He asked. "Who do you say I am?"

Simon Peter answered, "You are the Christ, the Son of the Living God."

Jesus replied, "Blessed are you, Simon son of Jonah, for this was not revealed to you by man, but by My Father in heaven. And I tell you that you are Peter, and on this rock I will build My church, and the gates of hell will not overcome it. I will give you the keys of the kingdom of heaven; whatever you bind on earth will be bound in heaven, and whatever you loose on earth will be loosed in heaven" (Matthew 16:13-19).

I never realized until I went to Israel what a dark place Caesarea Philippi must have been in the days when Jesus was

Above and right: The Grotto, or cave, of Pan, contains many carvings where idols would have been set.

speaking.

The Temple of Pan had been built there a few hundred years earlier, and when people came to worship Pan, they would bring with them an infant child to be offered as a sacrifice. The child was thrown into the water that flowed from the rock on the side of the cliff. If the child went under the water and disappeared, that meant Pan had accepted their sacrifice. If instead, the child's was dashed apart under water and its blood flowed into the river below, Pan had rejected their sacrifice. Either way, the child's life was over.

Not only was this area known for this pagan temple, but the Israelites had also rejected God in this region hundreds of years before that. Way back in the days of King Jeroboam, Jeroboam ruled Israel from this area. But for fear that the people would want to leave his kingdom and side with the breakaway kingdom of Judah, he erected two altars in this area instead. He made two golden calves and said to the people:

Below: It seems fitting that Christ, in the shadow of this massive rock, would have renamed Simon to Peter (which means "rock"), saying, "I tell you that you are Peter, and on this rock I will build My church."

גשר רומין
ROMAN BRIDGE

Left: A Roman bridge at Caesarea Philippi, above which was the road leading to Damascus, the route which Paul would have taken when he experienced his dramatic conversion.

"It is too much for you to go up to Jerusalem. Here are your gods, O Israel, who brought you up out of Egypt." One he set up in Bethel and the other in Dan. And this thing became a sin; the people went even as far as Dan to worship the one there (1 Kings 12:28b-29).

So this region of Dan, at the northernmost border of Israel, which is so beautiful and hilly and rich on the outside, had been a place of great darkness spiritually. In Jesus' day, with the Temple of Pan located there, it was an even darker place. Yet this is where God chose to reveal to Peter and the other disciples that Jesus was the Christ. The darkness wasn't a problem for Him, for He was, as He called Himself, "the light of the world." Jesus said:

"I am the light of the world. Whoever follows me will never walk in darkness, but will have the light of life" (John 8:12).

Perhaps you're in a dark time or a dark place in your life today. Or perhaps you have family or friends who are surrounded by darkness. If so, I want to encourage you to take heart: Jesus can reveal Himself even in the darkest of times and places. In fact, based on the time and place where He made this revelation to Peter, Jesus seems to delight in doing just that.

I also want to encourage you to make sure your faith in Christ is profoundly personal. By that I mean, don't just take someone else's word for it that Jesus is the Christ, the Son of the living God. Make sure that this is something that you believe deeply yourself. If you look at Jesus' questions in the passage above, you'll see that He started by asking His disciples what others said about Him. "Who do people say that I am?" The disciples replied:

"Some say John the Baptist; others say Elijah; and still others, Jeremiah or one of the prophets."

It's sometimes safe and easy to talk about Jesus in terms of what others believe about Him. If asked who He is, some people might say, "Well, my grandmother thinks He's God, " or "My parents believe He's the Messiah," or "My friends say that He's their Savior." But after Jesus asked the disciples what others said about Him, He turned to them directly and asked who they thought He was.

"But what about you?" He asked. "Who do you say I am?"

There comes a point in life when you can no longer rely solely on the faith of others to get you through the trials you're facing. You can no longer waver between what others say about Christ. My prayer is that you'll be able to say, like Peter said:

"You are the Christ, the Son of the Living God."

"The Christ" (Greek) and "the Messiah" (Hebrew) both mean the same thing: "the Anointed One."

If you've never put your faith in Jesus, trusting and believing that He is the Christ, the Messiah, the Anointed One, the One who came to die for your sins and bring light into your world, I encourage you to do it today. And if you've already put your faith in Christ, know that He is a Savior who delights in revealing Himself even in the darkest of places. Keep on praying that He will reveal Himself again and again to you, to your family and friends, and to the rest of the world.

Let's pray:

Father, thank You for revealing that Jesus is indeed the long-awaited Messiah, the Savior of all who put their faith in Him. Help us to see that revelation for ourselves in a fresh way today, and help others see Him that way as well, no matter how dark it may seem all around them right now. In Jesus' name, Amen.

Below: The Banias, one of the four head waters that spring from underground to form the Jordan River.

Lesson 10

WHAT HAPPENED AT THE JORDAN RIVER?

For today's message, I'd like to take you to one of the world's most famous rivers, the Jordan River in Israel. The waters of this river flow about 200 miles from the north of Israel to the south, passing through the Sea of Galilee in the north, then continuing its final destination at the Dead Sea in the south. To find out some of the things that took place on this historic river, take a look at the short video at the link at the right that I shot on the banks of the river itself, then read on to hear about how very much God loves you—and how you can express your love back to Him.*

I've also posted another short video at the second link below of an actual baptism at the Jordan River, this one of my son Josiah. You'll note as you watch that there are some overly friendly fish in the river who love nibbling at people's toes! The fish are harmless, but they do make the baptism all the more... uhmm... exciting!**

So what happened at the Jordan River? This is where John the Baptist baptized Jesus. This is also where John the Baptist baptized thousands of people, as did Jesus' disciples.

*Watch "The Jordan River" on the Internet at this link http://youtube.com/watch?v=wjVvyDt5cBE and **YouTube.com/watch?v=1tpd-kQBQdo

Facing page and above: The Jordan River has served as the scene of many famous stories from the Bible, most notably the baptism of Jesus, and that of thousands of His followers, past and present.

Above: Joshua and the Israelites crossed over the Jordan when they entered Israel, the Promised Land, after coming out of slavery in Egypt.

The Jordan River has also been the site of many other events over several thousand years of history, such as:

• *when Joshua and the Israelites crossed the Jordan River on dry ground as they entered into the Promised Land (Joshua 3:14-17),*

• *when Naaman was healed of leprosy in the Jordan (2 Kings 5:8-14),*

• *when Elisha made an ax head float on top of the water (2 Kings 6:1-7),*

• *and when Elijah was taken up into heaven after crossing the Jordan with Elijah (2 Kings 2:6-12).*

But of all the events that took place in the Jordan, perhaps the most famous is the baptism of Jesus. And what makes that event so special to me is not just what Jesus did there, but what God the Father said to Jesus when Jesus was baptized there. Here's the story, as recorded in Matthew chapter 3:

Then Jesus came from Galilee to the Jordan to be baptized by John. But John tried to deter him, saying, "I need to be baptized by You, and do You come to me?"

Jesus replied, "Let it be so now; it is proper for us to do this to fulfill all righteousness." Then John consented.

As soon as Jesus was baptized, He went up out of the water. At that moment heaven was opened, and He saw the Spirit of God descending like a dove and lighting on Him. And a voice from heaven said, "This is My Son, whom I love; with Him I am well pleased" (Matthew 3:13-17).

I love the fact that God, the Father, told Jesus, His Son, how very much He loved Him—even before Jesus did one miracle, before He healed anyone of any disease, before He preached any sermon, walked on the water, or raised anyone from the dead.

God, the Father, loved Jesus, not because of all that Jesus had done for Him, but because Jesus was His Son.

And the truth is, God loves you for the same reason, not because of all you've done for Him, but simply because you're His son or daughter, made in His image, and created for a loving relationship with Him from the moment He conceived you (which, by the way, could have been long before the time that your parents conceived you...see Jeremiah 1:5, for example). God loves you. He adores you. He created you. And He has so much in store for you and your life.

The good news is you don't have to go to the Jordan River to let God love on you. He's glad to soak you in His love wherever you may be. How can you feel God's love more in your life? One way is to just take a few minutes to sit and meditate on the truth that He does indeed love you. Read

the passage of Jesus' baptism again from Matthew chapter 3 and remember that He loves you just as He loved Jesus, even before Jesus began His ministry.

Remember that you're His child, His little one, His beloved. Remember that He sent Jesus to die for the sins in your life, the messes that you've made, so that you won't have to pay the price for those sins yourself. Remember that His love

Right and above: Yardenit, at the southwestern end of the Sea of Galilee, serves as a popular baptismal site along the Jordan, providing towels, robes, and showers for those wishing to express their faith in Christ through baptism.

extends for generations to those who love Him. And remember that you really are special, a wonderful creation of the most loving Father in the world.

And while you're considering this passage on Jesus' baptism, can I also encourage you that if you've never been baptized to consider being baptized soon? There's something special that comes from being obedient to the Lord's command in this area. Jesus' words about baptism were so important that He included them in His final instructions to His disciples before going into heaven. Jesus said:

"Therefore go and make disciples of all nations, baptizing them in the name of the Father and of the Son and of the Holy Spirit, and teaching them to obey everything I have commanded you" (Matthew 28:19).

I've studied the topic of baptism for many years, yet I can honestly say that I still don't understand it fully. But what I do understand is that something powerful takes place when a person is baptized in the name of the Father and of the Son and of the Holy Spirit. I've seen baptism can touch people in so many ways, from realizing that they truly are saved and going to heaven, to feeling like their sins are dripping off of them as they come out of the water, to receiving new giftings

Left: Whether someone is baptized in the Jordan for the first time, or as a renewal of their faith in Christ, being baptized in the same river as Jesus brings the Bible to life in a special way.

from God to help them make the most of their new lives in Christ.

As a follower of Christ, baptism is one of those steps that demonstrate you are willing to follow in His footsteps, being baptized as He was baptized and then living the rest of your life as He lived His.

Let's pray:

Father, thank You for loving us even before we ever did anything for You, and regardless of *anything that we've done against You. We pray that You would pour out Your love on us again today in a way that we can hear it, see it, feel it, or otherwise sense it. Lord, we also pray that You would show us ways that we can express our love back to You, whether it is by being baptized ourselves, or in some other way, for our desire is to pour out our love on You as well. In Jesus' name, Amen.*

Below: Whether its the water, the hair, or the photographer, the Jordan River seems to have a "halo effect" on those who are baptized in it!

Lesson 11

WHAT WILL HAPPEN
AT THE DEAD SEA?

The Dead Sea was one of my favorite stops on our trip to Israel. Maybe it was because we had some extra time to relax there because of a change in our schedule. Or maybe it was because the land and the water were so unusually beautiful. But I think the main reason I liked it so much is because of what will happen there in the future. To see what it looks like yourself, and to find out what God is going to do there one day, take a look at this short video at the link at the right.* Then read

on to find out what God could do in your life in unexpected ways as well.

So what will happen at the Dead Sea? Everything will come back to life! To understand how dramatic this change will be, you have to understand how dead the Dead Sea really is.

The Dead Sea is the lowest spot on earth at almost 1,400 hundred feet below sea level. It's also the saltiest body of water on earth, with a salinity of 30-33%, which is about six to seven times saltier than the oceans. Because of this, and whatever other reasons God has

*Watch "The Dead Sea" on the Internet at this link http://youtube.com/watch?v=AU7fzzl6zOo

Facing page and above: The Dead Sea has the distinction of being both the lowest spot on earth and the saltiest body of water. But it hasn't always been—nor will it always be—dead!

Above: Signs in the wilderness, written in Hebrew, Arabic, and English. Below: an oasis of life springs up near the well-watered hotels at the Dead Sea.

There are no dead fish on the shore and the water is as clear as crystal, giving a clear view of millions of shimmering crystals of salt that cover the bottom of the sea itself. In the Bible, it's not called the Dead Sea, but rather the "Sea of Salt," which is perhaps is a bit more descriptive. It's also referred to as the Eastern Sea, as it is on the East side of Israel, and just southeast of Jerusalem.

Given this background of just how desolate the sea is, it's even more remarkable to read about what God is going to do there one day. You can read about it in the book of Ezekiel, chapter 47. God gave Ezekiel a vision of the future, showing him the new temple that would one day be in Jerusalem. And out from beneath this temple, a river would flow—a river of life, all the way to the Dead Sea. Ezekiel says:

chosen, nothing is able to live in the Dead Sea whatsoever. There are no fish in the water, so there are no birds in the air. There's no grass along the shoreline, and no algae growing along its edges. The Dead Sea really is dead!

For some reason, I used to picture the Dead Sea as some kind of smelly swamp filled with dead things. But actually there's nothing "dead" in it.

Then he led me back to the bank of the river. When I arrived there, I saw a great number of trees on each side of the river. He said to me, "This water flows toward the eastern region and goes down into the Arabah, where it enters the Sea [the Dead Sea].

When it empties into the Sea, the water there becomes fresh. Swarms of living creatures will live wherever the river flows. There will be large numbers of fish, because this water flows there and makes the salt water fresh; so where the river flows everything will live. Fishermen will stand along the shore; from En Gedi to En Eglaim there will be places for spreading nets. The fish will be of many kinds—like the fish of the Great Sea [the

Mediterranean]. But the swamps and marshes will not become fresh; they will be left for salt. Fruit trees of all kinds will grow on both banks of the river. Their leaves will not wither, nor will their fruit fail. Every month they will bear, because the water from the sanctuary flows to them. Their fruit will serve for food and their leaves for healing" (Ezekiel 47:6b-12).

The prophet Zechariah also makes reference to this event, saying:

On that day living water will flow out from Jerusalem, half to the eastern sea [the Dead Sea] and half to the

Above and below: The plant life near the hotels at the Dead Sea quickly gives way to the barrenness of the mountains in the background.

Above and right: The hotels and the spa-type water at the Dead Sea make it a popular resort destination for Israelis and foreigners alike.

western sea [the Mediterranean], in summer and in winter (Zechariah 14:8).

When you're standing at the edge of the Dead Sea, it's awesome to consider that one day it will be teeming with life—that one day, living water will pour out from underneath the temple in Jerusalem to bring life to all the water touches, even filling this great basin of the Dead Sea with enough fresh water to bring this barren spot back to life.

Having read through many of the other prophecies in the Bible and visited the spots where they've already been fulfilled—such as the destruction of Sodom and Gomorrah that God foretold to Abraham and took place near here, or the birth of the Savior that God told Micah would take place in Bethlehem hundreds of years before Jesus was born —I'm reassured that what has been foretold about the Dead Sea, and its coming back to life again, will take place just as certainly.

And it shouldn't be surprising that God can bring things that have been dead back to life again. I've seen Him do it in my own life, giving me a new birth over twenty years ago when I thought I was headed for death, then giving me an abundant life instead. And I've seen God do the same thing in the lives of countless others as well, breathing new life into marriages that were officially dead, or bringing forth new life from wombs that doctors had declared physically dead.

I think of ministries and churches and corporations that have been on the brink of bankruptcy, without a hope in the world, but through hope in God have come back to life more fully and fruitfully than ever.

God specializes in bringing the dead back to life! This isn't to say that God wants everything to live, for there are some things that should die in our lives, and other things that have run their course and need to pass on so that something fresh and new can be birthed. But there's no doubt that God can breathe life into anything that He intends to bring back to life!

Maybe there's something in your life right now that feels like it is dead or dying and you see no way in the world for it to come back to life. But don't put your hope in the world. Put your hope in the Lord God Almighty, the Author and Sustainer of life itself!

Before you give up on that which may look dead today, consider Him who

gives life and breath to every living thing that you see around you today. Be encouraged that the same God who raised Jesus from the dead can give life to your mortal bodies as well. Be encouraged that the same God who breathed life into Adam, who was made out of the dust of the ground, can breathe new life into your family, your business, your marriage, your ministry. Be encouraged that the river of life that will flow into the Dead Sea will bring life to all that it touches.

God loves to bring that which is dead back to life! Let His river of life flow into your life today!

Let's pray:

Father, thank You for showing us how you can breathe life into the most desolate places on earth, and encourage us that Your river of life can touch our lives as well. Lord, help us to have the faith that You can and You will bring new life back into everything that You have said should come back to life. In Jesus' name, Amen.

Right: The Dead Sea at dusk.

Lesson 12

WHAT HAPPENED AT
SODOM AND GOMORRAH?

I'm not usually a "fire and brimstone" type of preacher. But if there was ever a time to preach a message on fire and brimstone, it's today, because today we're going to look at the time when God rained fire and brimstone down from heaven on the cities of Sodom and Gomorrah because their wickedness had become so great. To find out what happened there, take a look at this short video at the link at the right, then read on below to learn how powerful God really is, and how God can use that power in your life today.*

So what happened at Sodom and Gomorrah? God destroyed them completely. The destruction that took place at Sodom and Gomorrah was so complete that nothing has grown again in that region for thousands of years.

Compare that to the most powerful destruction men have invented, such as the atomic bombs which destroyed the cities of Hiroshima and Nagasaki during the war with Japan, and you'll see just how powerful God really is.

*Watch "Sodom and Gomorrah" on the Internet at this link http://youtube.com/watch? v=UMzT_fK7U4c

Facing page and above: The region of Sodom and Gomorrah was once lush and well-watered, "like the garden of the Lord," but it was destroyed when God could not find even ten righteous people living there.

Above and facing page: When humans have destroyed cities with their most deadly devices—nuclear bombs—life springs back within a few decades. But when God destroyed Sodom and Gomorrah with His power, nothing has sprung back yet, even after after 4,000 years.

life again. Buildings, trees, and people had grown up all around them. I'm told that except for the monuments that were erected to remind people of the horrific destruction that took place there years ago, visitors may not even realize the cities were once destroyed.

Sodom and Gomorrah, on the other hand, have never come back to life, and it's not been just forty years, or four hundred years, but more than four thousand years.

While the cities themselves no longer exist, the memory of what happened there is often repeated. Abraham talked about Sodom and Gomorrah, as did Isaiah, Paul, Peter, John, and even Jesus. As for the condition of the land beforehand, we're told that it wasn't always a barren wasteland, but it was at one time *"well-watered, like the garden of the Lord" (Genesis 13:10)*. It

When the bombs were dropped on those cities, they were almost completely wiped out within seven seconds. But if you visited those cities just forty years later, although you would have found those cities had changed, you would have also found that they were teeming with

was such a desirable land that Lot chose to live there when Abraham gave him his choice of where to live.

But as desirable as the land may have been, the people of the land left much to be desired. Their wickedness had become so great that God sent two angels—in the form of men—down to Sodom to destroy it.

Although God's patience is longer than ours, even His patience runs out. And that time had come for Sodom. God didn't want to have to destroy it. He even told Abraham He would spare the entire city if He could find even ten righteous people living there. But when the angels arrived and went to spend the night with Lot and his family, the men of the city showed how far their wickedness had gone. The Bible says:

Before they had gone to bed, all the men from every part of the city of Sodom—both young and old—surrounded the house. They called to Lot, "Where are the men who came to you tonight? Bring them out to us so that we can have sex with them" (Genesis 19:4-5).

Lot pleaded with them not to do this to his guests, but the men of Sodom persisted, saying:

"Get out of our way. This fellow came here as an alien, and now he wants to play the judge! We'll treat you worse than them." They kept bringing pressure on Lot and moved forward to break down the door (Genesis 19:9).

No matter what you might think about the topic of homosexuality, the idea of men forcibly having sex with other men

goes against God's beautiful design for sex.

Through a miraculous intervention of the two angels, God whisked away Lot and his family, and finally did what He hoped He wouldn't have to do. Genesis 19:23-26 says:

"Then the LORD rained down burning sulfur on Sodom and Gomorrah—from the LORD out of the heavens. Thus He overthrew those cities and the entire plain, including all those living in the cities—and also the vegetation in the land. But Lot's wife looked back, and she became a pillar of salt" (Genesis 19:24-26).

Although Lot and his two daughters escaped, Lot's wife looked back, against the clear instruction of the angels who helped them to escape. Perhaps she hesitated and looked back to take one last look at the city where

she had spent so much of her life. Or maybe she was just curious and wanted to see for herself just how what such destruction might look like. But whatever the reason, her looking back caused her to suffer the same fate as those who had also so deliberately gone against God's commands—commands that were not designed to restrict or limit them, but commands that would help them to live, and live abundantly.

When Jesus talked about the destruction of Sodom and Gomorrah, He warned people:

"Remember Lot's wife!" (Luke 17:32).

I want to encourage you today to do the same: Remember Lot's wife!

I know that some of you are playing with fire. You're doing things that you know are against God's will for your life. Whether you're doing them because you've always done

them, or whether you're just curious and want to see what it's like, you're still playing with fire. And God's fire can burn you seriously—and for eternity.

God may have been patient with you this far and not yet brought the complete destruction upon you that He could bring at any moment. But don't mistake God's patience as His approval of what you're doing. The purpose of His patience is to give you time to turn from your sin so that you can save yourself from the destruction that's coming upon you if you don't.

Remember Lot's wife! Turn from the coming destruction while you still have a chance. Do it today. Don't hesitate. Don't look back. Don't let curiosity kill you. If you've been looking at pornography, stop it today. If you've been considering, or engaged in, and adulterous relationship, end it today. If you've been abusing drugs or alcohol, stop it today. If you've been using God's gift of sex in ways that are selfish

instead of ways that lead to an abundant life, stop it today. Remember Lot's wife, and live!

Let's pray:

Father, thank You for reminding us of Your incredible power and Your incredible patience with us. Lord, help us to throw off everything that hinders us from beautiful relationship with You and with those around us. Fill us with Your power to do all that You've called us to do today. In Jesus' name, Amen.

Facing page and right: While some might wonder if the destruction of Sodom and Gomorrah ever really happened, the land itself—and the words of men like Abraham, Paul, Peter, John, and Jesus—testify to its reality.

Lesson 13

WHAT HAPPENED AT MASADA?

In America, the "Fourth of July" is not just a date on the calendar, but to us is a phrase that is synonymous with the word "Freedom!" In Israel, there's a place called Masada that symbolizes for many Jews the fight for freedom as well, a fight that took place there back in 73 A.D.

To find out what happened and take a look at the mountain of Masada yourself, take a look at this short video at the link at the right.* Then read on to find out how taking a stand for freedom

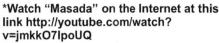

can inspire and impact those around you as well.

So what happened at Masada? This is the place where almost 1,000 Jews committed suicide. As gruesome as it may sound, the truth is that these people were so committed to the idea of staying free that they preferred to die free than to live as slaves.

Although the story of Masada doesn't appear in the Bible, and the suicidal aspects of the story go against traditional Jewish beliefs, what happened at Masada

*Watch "Masada" on the Internet at this link http://youtube.com/watch?v=jmkkO7lpoUQ

Facing page and above: The steep cliffs of Masada made it a venerable mountain fortress. Only the Roman Army, with plenty of time and thousands of tons of dirt, were able to breech it.

Left and above: Many buildings, rooms, and even mosaic floors have been unearthed at Masada from the time of King Herod.

still makes a profound statement about the lengths people are willing to go for freedom. In some ways, it reminds me of Patrick Henry's famous words at the beginning of the American Revolution: "Give me liberty, or give me death!"

But while Patrick's Henry's speech was a call to fight for the freedom in which they believed, for the 960 Jewish rebels who had been holed up in the mountain of Masada as a fortress from which they launched their attacks on the Roman Empire, fighting was no longer an option. The Romans had sent thousands of troops to Masada to take back this fortress that King Herod and others had developed over the years. (The word "masada" means "fortress.")

Because of the steep cliffs that protected Masada from its enemies, the Romans could not simply rush into the fortress to take it back. Instead, they moved tons of sand and dirt over the period of three years to build a siege ramp from the base of the mountain to its top. The ramp, as well as the remains of the Roman camps that were built in those days to house the armies for those three years, can still be seen clearly today.

It was a massive undertaking by the Roman government that finally culminated in the year 73 A.D., within a generation after the time when Jesus Christ had lived and died.

But when the Romans finally reached the top of Masada and broke through the gates, they found that the battle for which they had prepared for so long would not have to take place. The 960 rebels had, days earlier, realized that a fight would not be profitable. And rather than giving up their freedom to worship God in the way they believed, they gave up their lives, dying free, rather than living as slaves under Roman rule.

The story of their faith and how they came to their final end was documented by those who lived inside Masada. Interestingly, as a way to avoid committing wholesale suicide which was against their own teachings, each man drew lots and took turns taking the lives of their own families and friends, until finally only one man remained who alone killed himself.

While there's nothing scriptural to justify suicide, this story serves as a reminder of just how precious freedom really is, and to what lengths people will go to get it, rather than to live in slavery any longer.

It was the same sort of commitment the men who signed the U.S. Declaration of Independence made when they wrote:

"...we mutually pledge to each other our lives, our fortunes and our sacred honor" (from the final sentence of the Declaration of Independence).

And many of those who signed the Declaration of Independence did give up their lives and fortunes because of that pledge of sacred honor to one another.

Christ calls us to do the same.

Jesus frequently invited people to "come and see" what the kingdom of heaven was all about, then challenged them to go deeper and to "come

Above: The Romans built this siege ramp to advance to the top of Masada (looking down on the mound of dirt from above). Below: Remains of the huge Roman army camp at the base of Masada are still visible.

Above: A long, winding"snake path" has been the only way to ascend Masada for the past several thousand years, until a cable car system was recently installed (right), now whisking visitors to the top in minutes.

and die" for that kingdom of heaven.

Here are a few of the things that Jesus said about the cost of freedom that could come to those who follow Him:

"For whoever wants to save his life will lose it, but whoever loses his life for Me and for the gospel will save it" (Mark 8:35).

"If anyone would come after Me, he must deny himself and take up his cross daily and follow Me" (Luke 9:23).

"And everyone who has left houses or brothers or sisters or father or mother or children or fields for My sake will receive a hundred times as much and will inherit eternal life" (Matthew 19:29).

Jesus wants us to be as committed to Him and to the freedom that He offers as were those who were committed to freedom at Masada, as were those who were committed to freedom in America.

There's a price to pay for freedom that Christ offers. But when you're following Christ, any price is worth it. And once you're willing to die for Jesus, you'll find it's so much easier to live for Him as well.

Let's pray:

Father, thank You for dying for us to set us free, and help us to be willing to die to set others free as well. And Lord, help us realize that being willing to die for You will free to us to live for You even more. In Jesus' name, Amen.

Right: Our local Israeli guide taught us from the Bible—and from her extensive notes gathered over the years. Below: Our group pauses to take a picture-in-silhouette at the top of Masada.

Lesson 14

WHAT HAPPENED AT
THE QUMRAN CAVES?

The Qumran Caves are the site of what has been called "the greatest archaeological discovery of modern time." To find out what was discovered there, take a look at this short video at the link at the right.* Then read on to see how this tremendous discovery can affect your life in profound ways today, too.

So what happened at the Qumran Caves? That's where the Dead Sea Scrolls were found. And the scrolls found at Qumran aren't just any old scrolls. They contain the oldest hand-written manuscripts of the Hebrew Bible, or the Old Testament, that have ever been found.

Because the scrolls were made of animal skins and parchment, both of which are easily carbon-dated, the ages of these scrolls have been reliably dated as having been written between the years of 200 BC and 68 AD.C and 68 AD. It was quite a find for the shepherd boy who discovered the caves and the scrolls back in 1947, and for the many scholars and archaeologists who have found more caves and

*Watch "Qumran Caves" on the Internet at this link http://youtube.com/watch?v=tlWCOdgzEkg

Facing page and above: A community of believers in Qumran preserved the biblical scrolls in these caves. The copy of Isaiah predates any previously discovered copy of Isaiah by about 1,000 years.

Above: The Dead Sea Scrolls were first discovered here when a shepherd accidentally stumbled upon them in a long-covered cave. Dozens of other caves—and thousands of scroll fragments—have since been found nearby.

more scrolls in the Qumran area since that time.

Among the thousands of scrolls and scroll fragments that have been found, at least a portion of every book of the Old Testament has been discovered to date, with the exception of the book of Esther. Multiple copies of some of the scrolls have been found, such as the books of Psalms, Genesis, and Deuteronomy, and some of the books have been found in their entirety, such as the book of Isaiah.

What makes this discovery so exciting to researchers is that the books are so very old. For instance, the Isaiah scroll is 1,000 years older than any previously discovered copy of Isaiah. And even more exciting is the high level of accuracy of today's translations of the Bible when compared to these scrolls from the time of Christ.

Archaeological finds like those at the Qumran Caves continue to shed light and credibility on the Scriptures that we use today. In the words of the book of Isaiah itself:

"The grass withers and the flowers fall, but the Word of our God stands forever" (Isaiah 40:8).

When you look out at the barren mountains that surround Qumran, and see how the grass has withered, the flowers have fallen, and even the people who lived there have faded away, it's an awesome thought to think that the Word of God still stands.

The fact that God's Word has remained true for all this time confirms to me that the same words He spoke to the people back then, God wants to speak to you today.

When God says in the book of Jeremiah,

"I have loved you with an everlasting love," *(Jeremiah 31:3).*

He meant it then, and He means it today.

When God says in the book of Joshua,

"I will never leave you nor forsake you," *(Joshua 1:5),*

He meant it then, and He means it today.

When God said in the book of Isaiah,

"...those who hope in the LORD will renew their strength. They will soar on wings like eagles; they will run and not grow weary, they will walk and not be faint" *(Isaiah 40:31).*

He meant it then, and He means it today.

God loves you, He will never leave you nor forsake you, and He will give you the strength you need to fulfill the purpose for which He created you, if you'll continue to put your hope and faith in Him.

Even though the grass withers and the flowers fade away, the Word of God will stand forever, as evidenced once again by the ancient scrolls that were found in the caves at Qumran. God is faithful and true, and His Word is powerful and reliable.

Keep reading God's Word. Keep hiding it in your heart and memorizing it regularly. Keep meditating on it day and

Above right: The scrolls were preserved in pottery such as this large jar. Below right: Other pottery, displayed here at the Qumran National Park, was used for cooking, eating, and ceremonial cleansing.

night, as God told Joshua to do in Joshua 1:8. Don't let this ancient treasure that has been preserved for so long be wasted. Keep opening up your Bible again and again, and let God's Living Word breathe life into your daily walk with Him.

Let's pray:

Father, thank You for preserving these ancient manuscripts of Your Word for all of these years. Thank You for confirming to us that Your Word is reliable and true, and for giving us the inspiration we need to keep reading it, memorizing it and meditating on it day and night, so that we may experience the fullness of the life for which we were created. In Jesus' name, Amen.

Above: An aqueduct for the Qumran community was discovered for diverting fast-flowing, but infrequent, rain water into a series of pools for storage. Below left: Steps discovered at Qumran. Below right: Safety first, as provided by the Israeli Defense Force. Facing page: The view down the valley from Qumran to the Dead Sea.

Lesson 15

WHAT HAPPENED AT EN GEDI?

In the midst of the barren hills that surround the Dead Sea, there's a surprising oasis of life. It's called En Gedi, where a fresh water spring pours over steep crevices in the rock, creating a series of beautiful waterfalls and pools as the spring winds its way from the top to the bottom. To find out how God used this oasis to protect and provide for one of the most famous characters in the Bible, take a look at this short video at the link at the right.* Then read on

to learn how God can help you when you feel you are being treated unjustly.

So what happened at En Gedi? This is where David came to hide from King Saul when Saul was trying to kill David. But Saul wasn't always angry with David. In fact, David was one of Saul's favorites. David was called to come and live at the palace to play the harp for Saul, bringing great relief to the king every time David played.

But when David's fame began to grow as one of the best warriors in Saul's army, Saul became

*Watch "En Gedi" on the Internet at this link http://youtube.com/watch?v=o0yuzKFYLtU

Facing page: En Gedi is a literal oasis in the midst of the desert, with magnificent waterfalls that flow through an otherwise barren mountain pass. Above: The water bring flora and fauna to life.

Above: Wild goats, like this mountain Ibex, have inhabited the rocky crags of En Gedi since the days of King David, 3,000 years ago. Right: A pair of Ibex go head to head.

jealous. Fearing that the people would like David more than him, Saul tried to kill David by pinning him to a wall with his spear.

David tried to talk things out with Saul, reminding the king that David had never done anything wrong against him, but the conversations appeased Saul for only a short time. Then Saul was back to trying to kill David again because of Saul's burning jealousy. It soon became apparent that David would die if he stayed in the palace any longer.

So David fled. He went from place to place as Saul and his men tried to hunt him down. One of the places that God provided for David was En Gedi. The book of 1 Samuel says:

After Saul returned from pursuing the Philistines, he was told, "David is in the Desert of En Gedi." So Saul took three thousand chosen men from all Israel and set out to look for David and his men near the Crags of the Wild Goats (1 Samuel 24:1-2).

If you were to visit En Gedi today, you would see why David fled there. It featured an oasis of fresh spring water in the middle of the barren hills that surround the Dead Sea, with many caves in the hills where he could hide. It's an ideal spot to hide and be refreshed at the same time, and wild goats still climb the steep cliffs today, probably descendants from the wild goats for which the area was named back in David's time.

It was in one of these caves that Saul stopped for a bathroom break. In God's timing, it happened to be the very cave in which David and his men were hiding. The Bible says:

He [Saul] came to the sheep pens along the way; a cave was there, and Saul went in to relieve himself. David and his men were far back in the cave. The men said, "Today the LORD is saying, 'I will give your enemy into your hands for you to deal with as you wish.' Then David crept up unnoticed and cut off a corner of Saul's robe (1 Samuel 24:3-4).

But after cutting off the corner of Saul's robe, David was conscience-stricken that he should not do anything to harm the one that God had chosen as king, nor would he let any of his men attack Saul. When Saul left the cave, David followed after him and called out to Saul:

"My lord the king!" When Saul looked behind him, David bowed down and prostrated himself with his face to the ground. He said to Saul, "Why do you listen when men say, 'David is bent on harming you'? This day you have seen with your own eyes how the LORD delivered you into my hands in the cave. Some urged me to kill you, but I spared you; I said, 'I will not lift my hand against my master, because he is the LORD's anointed.' See, my father, look at this piece of your robe in my hand! I cut off the corner of

your robe but did not kill you. Now understand and recognize that I am not guilty of wrongdoing or rebellion. I have not wronged you, but you are hunting me down to take my life. May the LORD judge between you and me. And may the LORD avenge the wrongs you have done to me, but my hand will not touch you. As the old saying goes, 'From evildoers come evil deeds,' so my hand will not touch you. Against whom has the king of Israel come out? Whom are you pursuing? A dead dog? A flea? May the LORD be our judge and decide between us. May He consider my cause and uphold it; may He vindicate me by delivering me from your hand."

David did three things at En Gedi that I think are worth learning from when we feel we are being treated unjustly

First, he fled from a bad situation. While God may sometimes call you to stay in a bad situation to do all you can to work things out, there are still those times when it's truly OK to flee from it. David did his best to try to talk things out with Saul, but when it became apparent that his

Below: Caves like these dot the steep hills of En Gedi, making perfect hideouts for those not wanting to be found.

Above and right: The water that brings life to En Gedi also provides refuge for a variety of wildlife, including this rock hyrax, a type of badger.

very life was in danger if he stayed any longer, he fled. Jesus did the same thing at times, escaping quickly from people and places where people wanted to harm or kill Him, such as escaping from a crowd that wanted to throw Him over the cliff, or fleeing from those who tried to stone Him at the temple, or when He escaped the grasp of those who tried to kill Him as He walked through Solomon's Colonnade (see Luke 4:28-30, John 8:59, and John 10:39).

Second, David trusted God to protect and provide for him. Sometimes you may not want to flee from a bad situation because of the fear that something worse will happen to you. But if God is in it, He can protect and provide for you as well. God can provide a place for you like He provided En Gedi for David. It may not be like the place from which you came, but if it's God's provision, it can be just what you need, and a remarkable place in its own right. God protected and provided for the Israelites in the desert after they fled from their captors in Egypt, giving them manna and meat to eat for forty years. And He did the same for Elijah when Elijah fled from King Ahab, sending bread and meat to Elijah every morning and evening by way of birds who were directed by God to do so (see Exodus 16:35, Numbers 11:31-32, and 1 Kings 17:4-6).

Third, David trusted God to administer justice. Even though you may have a chance to administer justice yourself to those who wrongfully accuse or harm you, you may benefit by taking this lesson from David. He could have killed Saul himself, but then he would have had to face 3,000 angry troops next. By trusting the matter into God's hands, Saul was eventually punished for his wrongdoings, losing his life in battle, and David was brought back to live at the palace, this time as king. Even Jesus, for as many times as He escaped from the hands of His captors, trust God to administer the ultimate justice when God told Him to lay down His life for those who sinned against Him. Because of this, the Bible says:

Therefore God exalted Him to the highest place and gave Him the name that is above every name, that at the name of Jesus every knee should bow, in heaven and on earth and under the earth, and every tongue confess that Jesus Christ is Lord, to the glory of God the Father (Philippians 2:9-11).

Jesus trusted God to make things right in the end—and make things right He did—just like David trusted God, and just like you and I can do when we feel like others are treating us unjustly.

There are many other things you can do in situations like these, such as forgiving those who mistreat you (see Matthew 18:21-35) or calling for help from others who can step in and help with the situation (see Matthew 18:15-17).

Below: The view from En Gedi down to the Dead Sea. Right: The view from En Gedi up towards the mountains.

Whether you flee or whether you stay, whether the situation improves or gets worse, know that God can protect and provide for you in the midst of it, and that He can work all things for good in the end. Remember David at En Gedi, and remember what the Bible says:

"... that in all things God works for the good of those who love Him, who have been called according to His purpose" (Romans 8:28).

Let's pray:

Father, thank You for giving us the example of David and Saul, so we can learn from them to see just how much You can do for those who love You. And Lord, help us to to keep putting our trust in You that You will always work all things for good in Your way and in Your timing. In Jesus' name, Amen.

Lesson 16

What Happened
At Bethlehem?

Today we're headed to Bethlehem, the birthplace of Jesus. If you'd like to go with me into the Church of the Nativity and see for yourself the place underneath the altar of the church that has marked for centuries where they believe Jesus was born, take a look at this short video at the link at the right.* Then read on to learn why God might have chosen this place for the birth of His Son, and why having a heart like God's can bear fruit even hundreds—if not thousands—of

years later.

So what happened at Bethlehem? That's where Jesus was born.

The Church of the Nativity has marked the spot ever since 327 A.D., when the church was built at the request of Helena, the mother of Emperor Constantine. Helena was shown this spot on her visit to the Holy Land as the birthplace of her Savior, and she had a church built there to commemorate it. The spot had already been noted as the birthplace of Jesus for hundreds

*Watch "Bethlehem" on the Internet at this link http://youtube.com/watch?v=VohD_T_di40

Facing page: The pillars inside the Church of the Nativity are majestic, even though revealing the wear and tear of time, fires, and uprisings. **Above:** The bell tower, and homes on the hills of Bethlehem.

Left: The stage at the front of the Church of the Nativity contains a set of stairs on each side that lead down to the ground level. Candles mark a spot where the original manger is believed to have rested.

of years before that time by locals and historians alike, such as Justin Martyr in the 2nd century, and Origen of Alexandria in the 3rd.

It's amazing to think that Jesus was born on this spot, but it's even more amazing to think that Jesus was ever born at all. To think that God, the Father, would love us so much that He would send His Son into the world to live among us, to tell us of His love, and to demonstrate that love by giving up His life for us so we could live with God forever, that's what's really amazing.

As Jesus said so succinctly:

"For God so loved the world that He gave His one and only Son, that whoever believes in Him shall not perish but have eternal life" (John 3:16).

But why Bethlehem? Why did God want His Son to be born there? As with most things God does, God didn't pick the city of Bethlehem out of a hat of possible locations at the last minute. He had foretold it, hundreds of years earlier, through the prophet Micah:

"But you, Bethlehem Ephrathah, though you are small among the clans of Judah, out of you will come for me one who will be ruler over Israel, whose origins are from of old, from ancient times" (Micah 5:2).

But why? What was it about Bethlehem that made it so special that God would honor it in this way? I don't know for sure, but I do know that there was another man born in Bethlehem about a thousand years earlier about whom God had said:

"I have found David son of Jesse a man after My own heart; he will do everything I want him to do" (Acts 13:22b).

God honors those whose hearts are after His own heart: people who love God so much that they will do whatever He wants them to do, whenever He wants them to do it and however God wants them to do it.

And look what God did for David as a result:

"From this man's descendants God has brought to Israel the Savior Jesus, as He promised" (Acts 13:23).

I don't think it was haphazard that God chose Bethlehem as the birthplace of His Son. It seems to me that because David had honored God with his life,

Below: A star on the floor across from the manger has a hole in the ground, allowing visitors to reach through and touch the ground where Jesus would have been born.

Left and above: Manger Square leads visitors into the Church of the Nativity through a very small door, made that way deliberately to either encourage humility when entering the church—or to prevent invaders from rushing into it—or both.

God honored David with the life of His Son, even so many generations later.

Because of David's love for God, God seemed to move heaven and earth, and even the Roman Emperor, to orchestrate things so that this descendant of David's would be born back in David's hometown. As Luke records:

"In those days Caesar Augustus issued a decree that a census should be taken of the entire Roman world. ...And everyone went to his own town to register. So Joseph also went up from the town of Nazareth in Galilee to Judea, to Bethlehem the town of David, because he belonged to the house and line of David. He went there to register with Mary, who was pledged to be married to him and was expecting a child. While they were there, the time came for the baby to be born, and she gave birth to her firstborn, a son. She wrapped him in cloths and placed him in a manger, because there was no room for them in the inn" (Luke 2:1,3-7).

Above: The Star of Bethlehem, with its unique shape, stands atop Manger Square year-round.

Even the angels made the connection between Jesus' birthplace and David's, as one of them told the shepherds on the hills of Bethlehem that night:

"I bring you good news of great joy that will be for all the people. Today in the town of David a Savior has been born to you; He is Christ the Lord" (Luke 2:10b-11).

David was a man after God's own heart, and God honored his heart even a thousand years later. I pray you'll commit today to being a man or woman after God's own heart. You'll be blessed—and so will future generations who will be blessed through your faith.

Let's pray:

Father, thank You for sending Jesus to us here on earth, to live and die for us so that we could live with You forever. Help us commit to being men and women after Your own heart, so that we can bless Your heart, and the hearts of those in generations to come. In Jesus' name, Amen.

Below: Candles are lit throughout the day by visitors who stop to pray at an altar dedicated to the baby Jesus.

Lesson 17

WHAT'S THE CAPITAL OF ISRAEL?

We've been traveling all around the country of Israel during this study, but now we're going to focus on just one city for the remaining lessons: the capital city of Israel. To take a look this incredible place, and to see what the future holds for it, take a look at this short video at the link at the right.* Then read on to learn what happened there in the past and why what's going to happen there in the future is so important to us all.

So what's the capital of Israel? Jerusalem. Jerusalem became the capital of Israel in the year 993 B.C.—about 3,000 years ago—when King David moved from Hebron to Jerusalem. The Bible says:

"David was thirty years old when he became king, and he reigned forty years. In Hebron he reigned over Judah seven years and six months, and in Jerusalem he reigned over all Israel and Judah thirty-three years" (2 Samuel 5:4-5).

Jerusalem also became the spiritual capital of Israel at that time, for soon after King David arrived, he had the Ark of the Covenant brought into the city as well. If you remember from the book of Exodus, the Ark of the Covenant

*Watch "Jerusalem" on the Internet at this link http://youtube.com/watch?v=mKMqENBro7M

Facing page and above: The current flag of Israel bears the familiar six-pointed image of the Star of David. Jerusalem has been its capital since David moved there from Hebron about 3,000 years ago.

was an ornate wooden box covered with gold which contained the "covenant" between God and the Israelites in the form of the Ten Commandments, inscribed on two stone tablets by the finger of God Himself. God told the Israelites that He would make a dwelling for His name there above the ark, and that from there He would meet with them and speak with them (see Exodus 25:10-22).

So even though God certainly isn't confined to any one location, there was something special about this ark. When David's son, Solomon, built the temple in Jerusalem to house the Ark of the Covenant, Solomon said:

"But will God really dwell on earth? The heavens, even the highest heaven, cannot contain You. How much less

this temple I have built! Yet give attention to Your servant's prayer and his plea for mercy, O LORD my God. Hear the cry and the prayer that Your servant is praying in Your presence this day. May Your eyes be open toward this temple night and day, this place of which You said, 'My Name shall be there,' so that You will hear the prayer your servant prays toward this place. Hear the supplication of Your servant and of Your people Israel when they pray toward this place. Hear from heaven, Your dwelling place, and when You hear, forgive" (1 Kings 8:27-30).

Throughout the Bible, God said that He would choose a place for His Name, a place where His presence would rest, and that people should seek Him in that place and worship Him there. For instance, in Deuteronomy 12, God told the Israelites:

"You must not worship the LORD your God in their way. But you are to seek the place the LORD your God will choose from among all your tribes to put His Name there for His dwelling. To that place you must go; there bring your burnt offerings and sacrifices, your tithes and special gifts, what you have vowed to give and your freewill offerings, and the firstborn of your herds and flocks. There, in the presence of the LORD your God, you and your families shall eat and shall rejoice in everything you have put your hand to, because the LORD your God has blessed you" (Deuteronomy 12:4-7).

So when Solomon built the temple in Jerusalem, people came to worship there from all over, and continued to come for the next thousand years until the time of

Left: Jerusalem is known to many as the City of David, paying homage to King David's reign there.

Christ.

But when Jesus came, things changed. Jesus was, of course, Emmanuel, which means, "God with us." God, through His Son Jesus Christ, came to dwell among His people in real live flesh and blood. As the apostle John said so eloquently:

"The Word became flesh and made His dwelling among us" (John 1:14a).

And God's plan to dwell among His people didn't stop there. He said that He would continue to dwell among His people wherever they lived, even after Jesus' death and resurrection. Jesus talked about these coming changes in a conversation with a woman from Samaria. The woman said:

"Our fathers worshiped on this mountain, but you Jews claim that the place where we must worship is in Jerusalem" (John 4:20).

Jesus responded:

"Believe me, woman, a time is coming when you will worship the Father neither on this mountain nor in Jerusalem. You Samaritans worship what you do not know; we worship what we do know, for salvation is from the Jews. Yet a time is coming and has now come when the true worshipers will worship the Father in spirit and truth, for they are the kind of worshipers the Father seeks. God is spirit, and His worshipers must worship in spirit and in truth" (John 4:21-24).

Less than forty years after Jesus said these words, in the year 70 A.D., Jerusalem was attacked by the Romans and the temple was completely destroyed, never to be rebuilt again.

Jesus foresaw this coming destruction of Jerusalem, and when He did, He wept over the city. The Bible says:

"As He approached Jerusalem and saw the city, He wept over it and said, 'If you, even you,

Above: A statue of King David near his tomb, located beneath the Upper Room. David is remembered for being both a mighty warrior and a skillful harpist, playing soothing songs for King Saul, who reigned over Israel before him.

had only known on this day what would bring you peace—but now it is hidden from your eyes. The days will come upon you when your enemies will build an embankment against you and encircle you and hem you in on every side. They will dash you to the ground, you and the children within your walls. They will not leave one stone on another, because you did not recognize the time of God's coming to you'" (Luke 19:41-44).

Although the city was destroyed as Jesus foretold, and the temple along with it, God was not done making His dwelling among men. God said that He would send His Holy Spirit to live within all those who put their faith in Christ. And so it is that now through God's Holy Spirit He

Above: The Knesset is the current seat of government over Israel. Knesset means "the great assembly," and is made up of 120 leaders, a nod back to the time when 120 scribes, sages, and prophets ruled over Israel for the two centuries prior to the time of Christ.

away, and there was no longer any sea. I saw the Holy City, the new Jerusalem, coming down out of heaven from God, prepared as a bride beautifully dressed for her husband. And I heard a loud voice from the throne saying, "Now the dwelling of God is with men, and He will live with them. They will be His people, and God Himself will be with them and be their God. He will wipe every tear from their eyes. There will be no more death or mourning or crying or pain, for the old order of things has passed away" (Revelation 21:1-4).

It seems that God's greatest desire is to dwell among His people, to live with them, talk with them, walk with them, and make His home with them.

From the beginning of its days as the capital of Israel, Jerusalem has a long history of being the place where God dwelt among His people. And according to the Bible, the New Jerusalem will be a place where God will continue to dwell among His people—for the rest of eternity!

Here in the mean time, praise God that, through His Holy Spirit, He can still dwell among us anywhere, anytime, at any moment, day or night, when we put our faith in His Son, Jesus Christ.

If you've already put your faith in Christ, and invited His Holy Spirit to come and live within you, I want to encourage you to make the most of it. Worship God in spirit and in truth. Walk with Him. Talk with Him. Meet with Him

makes His dwelling among us. Now all of us can worship Him "in spirit and in truth," just as Jesus said, from anywhere in the world. As the apostle Paul said, now we are God's temple, and God's Spirit lives within each of us (see 1 Corinthians 3:16-17).

But back to Jerusalem, there is no doubt that God still has a special place in His heart for this Holy City, and that He has special plans for it still to come. God showed the apostle John what's to come in the future. John wrote:

"Then I saw a new heaven and a new earth, for the first heaven and the first earth had passed

every day and throughout your day. Recognize that God is with you right now and at all times. Remember that your body is a temple of the Holy Spirit and treat it with the utmost honor and respect. Then let God's Holy Spirit flow freely through your life into the lives of others, letting God use your hands, feet, eyes, ears, and heart as His to those around you. God loves you and He loves the fact that you would let Him come in and make His dwelling within you. Make the most of it!

And if you've never put your faith in Christ, do it today! God wants to make His dwelling within you, as well and give you access to His unlimited love and joy, peace and wisdom, from this day forward. Put your faith in Christ today. Ask Him to forgive you of your sins. Then invite His Holy Spirit to live within you starting today and on into eternity.

Let's pray:

Father, thank You for wanting to come and live with us. It's overwhelming to think that You would want to do that, yet we know that is Your greatest desire. Please, Lord, continue to make Your presence real to us again today, and know that we look forward to living with You forever one day in the New Jerusalem. In Jesus' name, Amen.

Below: Homes on the hillsides of Jerusalem today.

Lesson 18

WHAT HAPPENED ON MOUNT MORIAH?

Mount Moriah sits on what is perhaps the most valuable piece of real estate in the world. If it were for sale, I'm sure the price would be higher than anyone could pay. On some maps, it is marked as the center of the world, out of which everything else emanates. And in some ways, that's probably true. For it was here on Mount Moriah that some of the most important events of history took place—and will take place again in the future. To find out what happened here, take a look at the short video at the link below.* Then read on to see how what happened here can make a difference in what can happen in your life as well.

So what happened on Mount Moriah? This is where Abraham was going to sacrifice his son Isaac.

It's one of the first stories recorded in the Bible where someone expressed their great faith in God, even in the face of great obstacles.

God had promised Abraham that his descendants would be as numerous as the sand on the

*Watch "Mount Moriah" on the Internet at this link http://youtube.com/watch?v=qL-kjRbkeZ8

Facing page: Huge gates lead onto Mount Moriah, near the top of the Temple Mount, where God tested Abraham's faith. Above: Mount Moriah, as seen from the Mount of Olives, and from inside the gates.

seashore and as the stars in the sky. But there was one problem. Abraham didn't have any children. Not even one. And he and his wife believed that all hope was gone. At least until God spoke to them.

But how could God fulfill a promise like this? Yet Abraham believed Him, and God began to deliver on His promise by giving Abraham and Sarah a son from their own bodies.

But then, the tide seemed to turn. After believing God, and seeing the fulfillment of His promise begin, it seemed like God was about to go back on his promise. God told Abraham:

"Take your son, your only son, Isaac, whom you love, and go to the region of Moriah. Sacrifice him there as a burnt offering on one of the mountains I will tell you about" (Genesis 22:2).

It must have seemed ridiculous. If Abraham did what God said, not only was Abraham's son going to be dead,

but so was God's promise. But if Abraham felt any of that, the Bible doesn't record it. It simply says that early the next morning, Abraham saddled his donkey, cut some wood to make the offering, took two servants and his son Isaac, and set off for the place God had told him to go.

As he reached the spot, he built an altar, bound his son and put him on it. He took the knife in his hand, and just as he was about to slay his son, an angel of the Lord called out:

"Abraham! Abraham!"

"Here I am," he replied.

"Do not lay a hand on the boy," he said. "Do not do anything to him. Now I know that you fear God, because you have not withheld from me your son, your only son."

Abraham looked up and there in a thicket he saw a ram caught by its horns. He went over and took the ram and sacrificed it as a burnt offering instead of his son. So Abraham called that place The LORD Will Provide. And to this day it is said, "On the mountain of the LORD it will be provided."

The angel of the LORD called to Abraham from heaven a second time and said, "I swear by myself, declares the LORD, that because you have done this and have not withheld your son, your only son, I will surely bless you and make your descendants as numerous as the stars in the sky and as the sand on the seashore. Your descendants will take possession

Left: Detailed mosaics adorn the Dome of the Rock.

Above: The Dome of the Rock currently sits atop Mount Moriah, the enormous rock housed within it, and on which Abraham was asked to sacrifice his son, Isaac.

of the cities of their enemies, and through your offspring all nations on earth will be blessed, because you have obeyed me" (Genesis 22:11b-18).

Abraham had proved himself faithful. And so did God. When all hope seemed to be gone, Abraham still believed God could fulfill His promise, somehow, someway, sometime. And because of Abraham's faith, and God's faithfulness, Abraham's descendants are now counted in the millions, including those living today, and those who have lived over the past 4,000 years since this dramatic event on Mount Moriah.

The Dome of the Rock now stands on Mount Moriah over the massive rock rock where Abraham prepared to sacrifice Isaac.

It wasn't the only event that took place there. About a thousand years later, King David bought the threshing floor on

Above: Heavy doors guard the entrance to the famous rock contained within the dome.

Mount Moriah to build an altar and stop a plague that God had sent upon the people. When God saw David's faith, He proved Himself faithful again by stopping the plague after three days, just as He said He would.

About a thousand years after that, Jesus walked up to the steps of the temple to teach the multitudes, a temple that was built over this very place where Abraham and David had expressed their faith. He, too, eventually expressed his faith here, by willingly being sentenced to death in the chambers of the Antonia Fortress at the base of the Temple Mount, and carrying His cross from there to the hill where He died for all of our sins. And it was there that Jesus picked up his cross, and carried it to his death, the ultimate sacrifice that stopped the ultimate plague called "sin."

So you can see how this spot has been the site of many acts of faith, from Abraham 4,000 years ago, to David 3,000 years ago, and to Jesus 2,000 years ago. And you can see why this spot has also become priceless to millions, whether their heritage is Jewish, Muslim or Christian.

One day, the Bible says that a river of life will spring up from this spot. It will bring life to all that it touches, even the Dead Sea twenty miles away. While Mount Moriah may not have been a very peaceful spot over the years, it has been a spot where many acts of faith have played out, and where God has proven Himself to be faithful—over and over again, and where He will one day prove Himself to be faithful yet again.

How does this all relate to you? God loves it when people put their trust in Him, people whose hearts are fully committed to Him, in spite of how things might look around them.

Here's what the Bible says about Abraham:

"By faith Abraham, when God tested him, offered Isaac as a sacrifice. He who had received the promises was about to sacrifice his one and only son, even though God had said to him, 'It is through Isaac that your offspring will be reckoned'" (Hebrews 11:17-18).

Here's what the Bible says about David:

"I have found David son of Jesse a man after My own heart; he will do everything I want him to do" (Acts 13:22).

Here's what the Bible says about Jesus:

"Therefore God exalted Him to the highest place and gave Him the name that is above every name, that at the name of Jesus every knee should bow, in heaven and on earth and under the earth, and every tongue confess that Jesus Christ is Lord, to the glory of God the Father" (Philippians 2:9-11).

And here's what the Bible says about me and you, as written in Hebrews 11:6:

"And without faith it is impossible to please God, because anyone who comes to Him must believe that he exists and that He rewards those who earnestly seek Him" (Hebrews 11:6).

God wants you to have faith in Him, even when everything you see might tell you otherwise. God wants you to believe in Him, to trust in Him, to keep putting your faith in Him, no matter what, at all times, in all situations, believing that He exists, and that He rewards those who earnestly seek Him.

Keep putting your faith in God, and He'll prove Himself faithful to you, just like He proved Himself faithful to Abraham, David, and Jesus, right there on Mount Moriah.

Let's pray:

Father, thank You for showing your faithfulness to those who showed their faithfulness to You. Help us to be faithful to You today as well, believing that You exist, and that You will reward those who earnestly seek You. In Jesus' name, Amen.

Right: One of several doors that lead into the Dome of the Rock. Below: A close-up view of one of the marble slabs on the side of the dome reveals a rather haunting image.

Lesson 19

What's Happening At The Western Wall?

The Western Wall, also called the Wailing Wall, is one of the most famous places on earth, but not because of all that has happened there. The Wall is famous because of how close it is to something else. To find out what it's near, and what goes on there every day and why, take a look at this short video at the link at the right.* Then read on to find out how you can do the same thing they're doing at the Western Wall every day, wherever you are on the face of the planet.

So what's happening at the Western Wall? People are praying. They come here to pray from all over Jerusalem, from all over Israel, and from all over the world.

I was visiting a friend in New York before my first trip to Israel who said, "When you get to the Western Wall, will you say a prayer for me?" I said I would, even though I knew I could pray for him just as well right there in New York, which I did.

But I also knew why he wanted me to pray for him there, in that

*Watch "The Western Wall" on the Internet at this link http://youtube.com/watch?v=GYpVjid0RC8

Facing page and above right: People come from all over the world to say their prayers at the Western Wall of the Temple Mount. Above left: A model of the Temple Mount, and the walls around it.

Left and above: The Rabbinical tunnels have been excavated along the western edge of the Temple Mount, revealing the full length of the wall, down to the street level where Jesus would have walked.

spot: because the Western Wall is the closest spot to the Holy of Holies, the place where God chose—out of all the earth—as a dwelling place for His name.

You may have heard this famous quote from the Bible before:

"...if My people, who are called by My name, will humble themselves and pray and seek My face and turn from their wicked ways, then will I hear from heaven and will forgive their sin and will heal their land" (2 Chronicles 7:14).

But you may not remember the context in which those words were

spoken. The context was just after Solomon had finished building the Temple in Jerusalem as a place for God's name to dwell. Here's what God said to Solomon when the temple was completed:

"When Solomon had finished the temple of the LORD and the royal palace, and had succeeded in carrying out all he had in mind to do in the temple of the LORD and in his own palace, the LORD appeared to him at night and said:

"I have heard your prayer and have chosen this place for Myself as a temple for sacrifices.

When I shut up the heavens so that there is no rain, or command locusts to devour the land or send a plague among My people, if My people, who are called by My name, will humble themselves and pray and seek My face and turn from their wicked ways, then will I hear from heaven and will forgive their sin and will heal their land. Now My eyes will be open and My ears attentive to the prayers offered in this place. I have chosen and consecrated this temple so that My name may be there forever. My eyes and My heart will always be there' " (2 Chronicles 7:11-16).

So it's easy to see why people would want to go to the Temple Mount to pray still today. God promised that His eyes would be open and His ears attentive to the prayers offered in this special place.

And it's easy to see why the Temple Mount is still such a sought after property in the world: people want to be as close to God as they can get. They want Him to hear their prayers. They want Him to pay attention to their needs. People want God to answer their prayers, so they still try to get as close to the Temple Mount as they can to pray.

And that brings us to why the Western Wall is so important. The Temple Mount has changed hands many times over the years. Solomon's Temple was destroyed and rebuilt again, only to be destroyed again in 70 A.D. The domed building that now stands above the rock of Abraham was at one time a Christian church, with a cross atop the dome. There was also a time when an Israeli flag flew upon the Temple Mount. The dome is now adorned with a golden moon, the symbol of the Muslims who control the Temple Mount today. And as the third holiest site in Islam, it is forbidden for

Above: Some of the massive foundation stones that support the Temple Mount weigh as much as 200 elephants.

Jews or Christians to pray anywhere upon it—and if they are seen to be praying, they are asked to leave.

So today, the closest spot to the place where the Holy of Holies once was, and where Jews can pray, and Christians as well, for that matter, is the Western Wall, a 187 foot expanse of the wall that can be seen on the southwestern edge of the Temple Mount (the walls of the Temple Mount are not to be confused with the city walls that encircle the entire old city of Jerusalem, which Nehemiah rebuilt, and which are are further out).

But what many people don't realize is that the Western Wall extends along the full length of the Temple Mount, and can

Above: People not only pray at the Western Wall, but they'll often write their prayers on slips of paper, roll them up tightly, and place them into crevices within the wall itself.

be visited today in its entirety by descending into the rabbinical tunnels, an extensive network of tunnels that are said to extend underneath the entire Temple Mount as well. The tunnels along the Western Wall have been excavated in recent years, and you can go down underground and walk along the entire length of the Western Wall, down to what would have been the street level during the time of Jesus!

It is spectacular to walk along this massive wall at its base, with its huge foundation stones, and there is one spot along the wall that garners particular attention: the spot that is said to be directly across from where the Holy of Holies once stood, the place where the Ark of the Covenant was located (and is shown in the picture at the right, and in video above). It is remarkable to stand there and imagine that this is the closest we can get to the place where God chose for His name to dwell.

Having said all of that, there is a closer spot still where God has since chosen for His name to dwell: within the hearts of all those who have put their faith in His Son, Jesus Christ. As the apostle Paul told the Ephesians:

"I pray that out of His glorious riches He may strengthen you with power through His Spirit in your inner being, so that Christ may dwell in your hearts through faith" (Ephesians 3:16-17).

If you've put your faith in Christ, God's Spirit lives within you, just as Jesus told the disciples He would:

"If you love me, you will obey what I command. And I will ask the Father, and He will give you another Counselor to be with you forever—the Spirit of Truth. The world cannot accept Him, because it neither sees Him nor knows Him. But you know Him, for He lives with you and will be in you" (John 14:15-16).

We all long to be close to God. We want to be with Him and know that He is close enough to hear our prayers. A new worship song by Dennis Jernigan, called "Breathe," expresses this strong desire for intimacy with God by saying:

*"Lean so close that I feel You breathe
Lean so close You quench this thirst in me
Lean so close You loose these chains in me
Set me free... So I can breathe..."*

Imagine, leaning so close to God that you could feel Him breathe! The good news is that if you want to be this close to God, to talk to Him and to be sure that His eyes are upon you and His ears are attentive to your prayers, all you need to do is to put your faith in Christ. If you've already done that, you need look no further than within your own heart to find the place where the Spirit of God Himself now dwells.

Lean close to God today. Feel his breath on your cheek. Let Him whisper the words He longs to tell you, and the words you're probably longing to hear from Him as well: "My child, I love you." Then respond to that love with a few words of your own.

Let's pray:

Father, thank You for coming to dwell among us, both at the Holy of Holies and now within the temple of our own hearts. Lean so close to us so we can hear You, see You, feel You, touch You, and thank You for being there so we can lean upon You as well. In Jesus' name, Amen.

Below: These women are praying at a place along the Western Wall, deep inside the Rabbinical Tunnels, that is the closest they can get to the original Holy of Holies, the location where God said His name would dwell forever.

Lesson 20

WHAT HAPPENED AT THE NORTH GATE?

I'd like to tell you a very personal story today. It's about what happened to me at the North Gate of the Temple Mount. But before I tell you my story, I'd like to tell you Ezekiel's story, and what he saw, in a vision from God, at the North Gate of the Temple Mount. It's a beautiful picture of what it will be like when Jesus returns. Take a look at the short video at the link at the right to see where the northern gates of the Temple once stood.*

So what happened at the North Gate? That's where Ezekiel saw a vision of a river of life flowing out from the Temple, bringing life to all that it touched. It was a vision for him, but it will be a reality for us one day, when Jesus returns. You may remember some of Ezekiel's story from when we talked about the Dead Sea, when God showed Ezekiel this river flowing from the Temple and said:

> *"Fruit trees of all kinds will grow on both banks of the river. Their leaves will not wither, nor will their fruit fail. Every month they will bear, because the*

*Watch "The North Gate" on the Internet at this link http://youtube.com/watch? v=G0ggH5KHxBU

Facing page: The view through the northern gates on the Temple Mount. Above left: The gates as viewed from the dome. Above right: A large-scale model of the Temple Mount during Solomon's time.

Above: A fountain on the Temple Mount brings just a trickle of water compared to the rivers of life that will one day flow from beneath the altar that Ezekiel saw in his vision.

water from the sanctuary flows to them. Their fruit will serve for food and their leaves for healing" (Ezekiel 47:12).

But that wasn't the only vision Ezekiel had of what would happen at the Temple. God had brought him there many times over his years as a prophet to show him what would happen, ranging from bringing judgment on those who had forgotten God, to bringing blessings to those who continued to wait on Him.

God used one of Ezekiel's visions to speak to me one day. I'd like to share that story with you to encourage you that God still speaks today as He did in the days of Ezekiel.

It happened just shortly after I quit my secular job to go into full-time ministry. I felt God was calling me to do something full-time for Him, but I didn't know what. It was only a week or so after I had quit when I felt God calling me to the Holy

Land for the first time. As I prayed about the trip, I felt there were two places I should visit in particular: the place where the Temple used to be and the place where Jesus died. I asked God why He wanted me to go to these two places, and I felt He said: "I will reveal Myself to you there." So I had just finished writing these things down in my journal, which I was using during my prayer time with God, and was about to stand up to go on with my day, when I felt God say He wasn't done yet.

"Open your Bible," He seemed to say. So I opened it up and began to read the words I saw on the page. It was a passage from Ezekiel, chapter 8:

"In the sixth year, in the sixth month on the fifth day, while I was sitting in my house and the elders of Judah were sitting before me, the hand of the Sovereign LORD came upon me there. I looked, and I saw a figure like that of a man. From what appeared to be his waist down he was like fire, and from there up his appearance was as bright as glowing metal. He stretched out what looked like a hand and took me by the hair of my head. The Spirit lifted me up between earth and heaven and in visions of God he took me to Jerusalem, to the entrance to the north gate of the inner court, where the idol that provokes to jealousy stood. And there before me was the glory of the God of Israel, as in the vision I had seen in the plain" (Ezekiel 8:1-4).

There I was, thinking about going to the place where the Temple used to be in Jerusalem, and I felt like God was giving me very specific instructions about where to go on the Temple Mount. In Ezekiel's vision, he was picked up and transported to Jerusalem, between earth and heaven (by the hair of his head, no less!), and dropped him off at the entrance to the north gate of the inner court of the temple. It was there that God revealed His glory to Ezekiel.

I pictured my own upcoming flight to Israel, where I would be transported to Jerusalem, between earth and heaven (by plane, thankfully!) and heading to the Temple Mount as well. I felt like God was telling me for some reason to go specifically to the place where the north gate of the inner court of the temple would have been. Although the temple itself no longer exists, the location of the the north gate of the inner court was quite likely just to the north of the rock of Abraham, inside the Dome of the Rock, and where the Holy of Holies would have been located.

I stood up with renewed interest in whatever God wanted to reveal to me on this trip, and on that spot in particular. I went home and told my wife about what I felt God was saying, and that if she needed to find me in Israel, to look for me at the north gate on the Temple Mount!

You can imagine my frustration when I finally got to Jerusalem to find out that the Temple Mount was closed. It was the Muslims holy month of Ramadan, and I was told that the Temple Mount was closed off to non-Muslims. Each day of my trip, I went into Jerusalem and tried to get in, but each day I was turned away.

As I sat outside the walls of the city of Jerusalem one day, I read in my Bible about people who were anointed with oil when they went into service for God. I began to wonder if God could somehow anoint me with oil as I was going into service for Him as well. But where could

I find someone who would anoint me with oil? I couldn't just walk up to someone on the streets of Jerusalem and ask if they'd do it!

The next morning, however, as I was talking to a shopkeeper about my desire to see the Temple Mount, but my frustration that I kept getting turned away, he told me that if I went to a certain door before 9 a.m., I could get in, for tourists could get in for a few hours that morning if they went before 9. It was just before 9 a.m. when he told me, so I took off running for the door he had described. After a quick search of my backpack, the men watching that door let me in. I had made it onto the Temple Mount!

I headed for the Dome of the Rock and ran into a group of tourists who were going inside. One woman was staying behind to watch their pile of backpacks, shoes, and cameras, as none of those things could be brought into the Dome. She said she would watch my things, too, and I stepped inside the Dome.

Below: The base of the fountain sports a ring of water spigots and stone seats for foot washing.

I went to the north side of the wide rock inside, where Abraham was supposed to sacrifice Isaac, and I stood and thanked God for bringing me there. I asked Him to reveal anything that He wanted to reveal to me. I was ready to hear it. I noticed a man to my right who had climbed up on the short base of a pillar inside the door to get a better view of the rock from above. I continued my conversation with God, and after waiting a bit longer for anything He might say, but hearing nothing more, I went back outside.

I returned to the woman who was watching our pile of things, and she started to ask me a series of questions: why I had come, what I was doing there, what kind of church did I go to. I tried to politely answer her questions, but I was in a bit of a hurry to go and explore more of the Temple Mount. I was, after all, waiting for God to show up!

But she kept asking questions, and finally said, "My husband's a pastor, and he would love to hear all of this, but he's still inside the Dome. Could you wait till he comes out and tell him what you're doing?" So I waited.

When her husband came out, I saw that he was the same man I had seen inside the Dome on the north side of the rock of Abraham. I shared with him why I had come to Israel, and about some of my recent experiences, such as praying for the healing of a woman who had cancer. He asked, "When you pray for people, do you anoint them with oil?" He said he found it helpful to anoint people with oil when he prayed for them, as it says to do in the book of James.

I was stunned. I had just been praying the day before that God would send someone to anoint me with oil as I began my ministry, and here stood someone who just might do it, right at the place where the north gate of where the inner courts of the Temple would have been! I told them about my prayer, and asked if they might pray for me and anoint me with oil for my service to God. They said they'd be glad to, and although they didn't have any with them, they said we could buy some at one of the shops nearby. Then, when their group took their next break from their tour, they'd pray for me.

I followed them as they left the Temple Mount, walking through the actual northern gates of the Temple Mount that are there today. We walked along the Via Dolorosa, the path through the streets that Jesus was said to have taken when He carried His cross to His death. We ended up at the Church of the

Left and below: The sign that visitor's see when approaching the Temple Mount is written in both Hebrew (which is written from right to left) and English.

הקרן למורשת
הכותל המערבי
The Western Wall
Heritage Foundation

מבקר נכבד

1. הנך נכנס למתחם הכותל המערבי. למא
2. מבקרים עם קוצב לב: נא להודיע לנלא
3. בכניסה לכותל מופעלת מערכת בשבת
4. מערכת זו הותאמה לעבודה בשבת אישור
מכון צומת. המערכת קיבלה בהם אין חש
ופוסקי הלכה כי לעובר העינוו הננ
למען ביטחונך ובטחון הציבור המ
ל.... הורואות להישמע

Dear visitors

1. You are entering the Western Wall Piaza.
2. Visitors with pace-makers should inform the security personnel.
3. Visitors must walk through a metal detector at the entrance to the Western Wall.
4. This system has be....

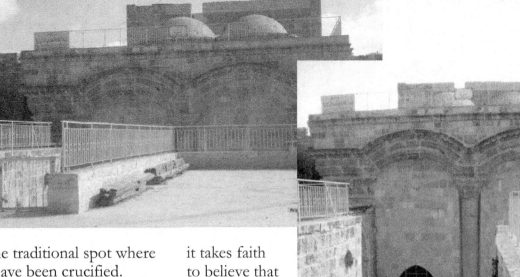

Right: The Eastern Gate, also called the Beautiful Gate, has been sealed for years in an attempt to prevent the Jewish Messiah from entering through it, as prophesied in Scripture.

Holy Sepulcher, the traditional spot where Jesus was said to have been crucified. Then their group took a break.

We went to a nearby shop and bought a small bottle of "Anointing Oil from the Holy Land," and went back inside the church to pray. It was there, at the place where Jesus died, that they—and God—anointed me with oil for the service I had recently begun for Him.

It was a holy moment, as I realized what God had done: He had brought me to the two places He put on my heart to come: the place where the Temple used to be and the place where Jesus died. And it was in those two spots where God revealed Himself to me in a very personal way, showing me how clearly He speaks, and how clearly He answers prayers. And it was in that moment that God ordained me for the ministry that I've now been doing for the past fifteen years.

As I flew home the next day, I thanked God again for speaking so clearly and personally to me, just as He has spoken to people throughout the ages. What an awesome God we serve!

I want to encourage you today to listen carefully for God's voice. He still speaks today, not just about "big" things, but about the every day things as well. But it takes time to hear Him clearly, and it takes faith to believe that what He says to you is true. Know, however, that God loves those who seek Him, and when you ask for wisdom, He will give it to you generously. As it says in the Bible:

"If any of you lacks wisdom, he should ask God, who gives generously to all without finding fault, and it will be given to him. But when he asks, he must believe and not doubt, because he who doubts is like a wave of the sea, blown and tossed by the wind" (James 1:5-6).

Take some time to listen to God today. Quiet your heart, open your Bibles, and ask Him your questions. Then get ready to receive whatever He has to say.

Let's pray:

Father, thank You for speaking to Ezekiel centuries ago, and thank You for speaking to us still today, through Your Word and by Your Holy Spirit. We pray that You would again answer the questions that are on our hearts today, and that we would have the faith to believe You when the answers come. In Jesus' name, Amen.

Lesson 21

WHAT HAPPENED AT
THE SOUTHERN STEPS?

Neil Armstrong was the first man to walk on the moon, yet he said that walking on the southern steps of the Temple Mount was even more exciting. Why? To find out, take a look at this short video at the link at the right, then read on to learn how you can have exciting moments like this every day.*

So what happened at the southern steps? That's where Jesus walked.

When Neil Armstrong visited Israel in 1994, he asked his host if there was a place where Jesus would have walked—without a doubt—2,000 years ago. His host, Archaeologist Meir Ben Dov and the excavator of the Temple Mount and southern walls in Jerusalem, answered that the southern steps were, for sure, the steps that Jesus would have used when He walked up to the Temple.

Mr. Armstrong bent down and kissed the ground, saying that this was an even more exciting moment for him than walking on the moon. If you were to go to Israel today and wanted to walk

*Watch "The Southern Steps" on the Internet at this link http://youtube.com/watch?v=XuMIH2krePk

Facing page and above left: These original steps that once lead up to the Temple Mount were in use during the days when Christ was alive. Above right. Excavations near the Southern Steps.

Above: Three arches, now sealed shut and barely visible here in the center of the wall, once lead worshippers up and into the Temple Mount complex.

It was on one of these trips that Mary and Joseph lost Jesus as they were traveling back home, thinking that He was traveling back with relatives or friends. After searching for Him for three days, they finally found Him, back in Jerusalem in the Temple Courts. He was sitting among the teachers, listening to them, and asking them questions. Upon hearing that His parents had been anxiously searching for Him, Jesus replied: *"Why were you searching for me? Didn't you know I had to be in my Father's house?" (Luke 2:49).*

Then as an adult, Jesus often taught crowds of people there at the Temple Courts. The Bible says that during the final week of His life:

"Each day Jesus was teaching at the Temple, and each evening He went out to spend the night on the hill called the Mount of Olives, and all the people came early in the morning to hear Him at the Temple." (Luke 21:37-38).

where you knew Jesus would have walked, you would go to the southern steps.

That's because the southern steps, which have been excavated in recent years, served as the main entrance to the entire Temple Mount complex. And we know from Scripture that Jesus went to the Temple several times throughout His life. The Temple itself has since been destroyed, and the Temple Courts are buried under years of civilization and rebuilding. But the southern steps can still be walked upon today.

The Bible says that Jesus first visited the Temple as a child, when Mary and Joseph brought Him here to be consecrated to the Lord (see Luke 2:21-40). The family then came back to Jerusalem year after year, as was their custom, for the yearly Feast of the Passover (Luke 2:41).

If just walking where Jesus walked sounds exciting—like it was to Neil Armstrong—imagine what it would have been like to hear Him speak! Imagine being there in person, back in 33 A.D., and listening to the words that Jesus spoke, coming from His own mouth!

Imagine hearing Jesus tell some of His parables for the very first time, right there in the Temple Courts: the parable of the two sons, or of the ungrateful tenants, or of the wedding banquet of a king.

Imagine Jesus answering people's questions, whether honest and practical questions, or those that were asked by people in order to trap Him, with words that astonished all who heard them and silenced His critics.

Imagine hearing Jesus answer the question about whether or not it was right to pay taxes to Caesar, and then hearing Jesus ask you to take out a coin with Caesar's image on it and saying:

"Give to Caesar's what is Caesar's, and give to God what is God's" (Matthew 22:21).

Or imagine Him answering the question about the resurrection of the dead, and whether or not people would really live again after they died, and hearing Jesus say:

"Have you not read what God said to you, 'I am the God of Abraham, the God of Isaac, and the God of Jacob'? He is not the God of the dead but of the living" (Matthew 22:31b-32).

Or imagine Jesus being asked what He thought was the greatest commandment in the law, and hearing Jesus say for the first time:

" 'Love the Lord your God with all your heart and with all your soul and with all your mind.' This is the

first and greatest commandment. And the second is like it: 'Love your neighbor as yourself' " (Matthew 22:37-38).

Or imagine watching, along with Jesus, as a poor widow passed in front of you and put two very small coins into the Temple offering, and hearing Jesus say:

"I tell you the truth, this poor widow has put in more than all the others. All these people gave their gifts out of their wealth; but she out of her poverty put in all she had to live on" (Luke 21:2-4).

All of these things took place at the Temple Courts. No wonder the Bible says that all those who heard Jesus speak there —even when He was just twelve—were

Right: Jesus said that one day the Temple would be destroyed, with not one stone left standing. This happened in 70 A.D. when the Romans destroyed the Temple completely, as confirmed by these stones from the Temple lying toppled at the base of the Temple Mount. Inset: This fallen stone was inscribed with the words, "To the place of trumpeting."

Left and above: Several baths for ritual cleansing have been found outside the Southern Steps, with stairs leading down into them for people to bathe before entering the Temple.

"...amazed at His understanding and His answers" (Luke 2:47).

No wonder the Bible says that the crowds who heard Jesus speak at the Temple Courts as an adult were *"...astonished at His teaching" (Matthew 22:33b).*

No wonder the Bible says that when He spoke during the feast that *"...all the people came early in the morning to hear Him at the Temple" (Luke 21:38).*

Maybe you wish you could have been one of those people who got up early in the morning to hear the wisdom of Jesus. The truth is, you *can* be one of those people!

If you'd like to sit at the feet of Jesus and listen to Him speak His words to you, words that are practical and words that answer the honest questions on your

heart, you can still do it today. You can pick up a copy of the Bible and read the words of Jesus, as recorded in the books of Matthew, Mark, Luke, and John, recorded by people who heard Him speak those words in person—Matthew, Mark and John—and Luke, who personally and thoroughly researched the stories by asking eyewitnesses who heard Jesus speak to verify their authenticity, people who were still living at the time he wrote his book. Some of you may even have "red-letter Bibles," where the words of Jesus are highlighted in red so that you can find them easier, underscoring the words of this master teacher that were spoken 2,000 years ago.

Thankfully, the words that Jesus spoke back then are just as applicable to our lives today. Jesus isn't a teacher who is now dead and silent. He's just as alive and eager to speak to you today as He was back then. As the Bible says:

"Jesus Christ is the same yesterday and today and forever" (Hebrews 13:8).

What a blessing it is to be able to walk where Jesus walked, as Neil Armstrong did, and what a blessing it would have been to hear Him teach in person at the Temple Courts. But what a blessing it is that we can still come to Him every day, whether early in the morning, throughout the day, or late in the day, and hear the wisdom of God as spoken through Jesus Christ Himself.

Come to Christ again today—and every day—and let Him speak His words of life to you.

Let's pray:

Father, thank You for sending Jesus to speak to the crowds at the Temple, and thank You for those who recorded His words so we can continue to hear Him speak to us today. Open our hearts to hear those words as we come to You again today and every day. In Jesus' name, Amen.

Below: The excavations at the Southern Steps now form an Archaeological Park, displaying many of the historical items found there.

Lesson 22

WHAT HAPPENED AT THE POOLS OF BETHESDA?

The Pools of Bethesda, just outside the Temple in Jerusalem, were said to have healing powers. But one day, when a man who had been ill for thirty-eight years went to the pools for healing, he discovered the Source of all true healing. To find out what happened that day, take a look at this short video at the link at the right, shot on location at the remains of the pools themselves.* Then read on for encouragement that God still heals today.

So what happened at the Pools

of Bethesda? That's where Jesus healed a man who had been ill for thirty-eight years.

The man had apparently come to the Pools of Bethesda looking to be healed by the waters there. According to local tradition, there were times when an angel of the Lord would stir up the waters in the pools, and the first one into the water after such a disturbance would be healed. As a result, the Bible says, *"Here a great number of disabled people used to lie: the blind, the lame, the paralyzed" (John 5:3).*

*Watch "Pools of Bethesda" on the Internet at this link http://youtube.com/watch?v=1My68QPc7io

Facing page and above left: The remains of the Pools of Bethesda, where Christ healed a man who had been lame for thirty-eight years. Above right: Saint Anne's Church, built near the pools by the crusaders.

Above: Many sick and lame people would gather daily at the Pools of Bethesda, waiting for the Spirit of God to bring them the healing they so desperately sought.

On one of Jesus' visits to Jerusalem, He went to the pools and saw this man lying there who had been sick for thirty-eight years. Jesus asked:

"Do you want to get well?" (John 5:6b).

The man must not have know who was asking him this question, for he simply replied that he had no one to help him into the pool when the water was stirred. Little did he know that he was talking to the One who is the Source of all healing! But he was about to find out. In the next moment, Jesus did for him the miracle that he had waited so long to receive:

"Then Jesus said to him, 'Get up! Pick up your mat and walk.' At once the man was cured; he picked up his mat and walked" (John 5:8).

Jesus is known for many things, but His ability to heal ranks right at the top. The Bible says,

"And wherever He went—into villages, towns or countryside—they placed the sick in the marketplaces. They begged Him to let them touch even the edge of His cloak, and all who touched Him were healed" (Mark 6:56).

As the "Author of Life," as Peter called Him, Jesus is the One who knows best how to heal a life. When God designed our bodies, He designed them with healing in mind, knowing that we wouldn't go through life unscathed. When doctors stitch up a wound or administer an antibiotic, they are often using techniques that simply tap into the body's God-given ability to heal itself, helping to stimulate, accelerate, or otherwise facilitate the body's built-in healing processes.

That's why God said to Moses:

"...for I am the Lord who heals you" (Exodus 15:26).

And God is a healing God not just of our bodies, but of our hearts, minds, and souls as well. After healing the man at the pools, Jesus later found him again at the Temple and said to him:

138

"See, you are well again. Stop sinning or something worse may happen to you." (John 5:14).

Jesus wanted the man to be fully healed, not just in part, but the whole; not just in body, but in heart, mind, and soul.

Jesus' healing power extends to all aspects of our lives. In Paul's letter to the Corinthians, he talks about people in the church there who had, in the past, suffered from all kinds of problems: sexual immorality, idolatry, adultery, prostitution, homosexuality, thievery, greediness, drunkenness, slandering and swindling. But Paul goes on to say,

"And that is what some of you were. But you were washed, you were sanctified, you were justified in the name of the Lord Jesus Christ and by the Spirit of our God" (1 Corinthians 6:11).

They were changed, healed, renewed, restored. How? In the name of the Lord Jesus Christ and by the Spirit of our God. All healing —whether physical, mental, spiritual or emotional—comes from God, in the name of the Lord Jesus Christ and through His Holy Spirit.

Even those healings performed by doctors or nurses, psychologists or psychiatrists, mothers or fathers, or friends or family, ultimately come from the God who designed our hearts, souls, minds, and bodies.

If you need a healing in your life today, or know someone who does, I want to encourage you, and for you to encourage them, to come to Jesus, the Author and Sustainer of life itself.

Remember the man who was healed at the pools of Bethesda. Jesus touched him and said, *"'Get up! Pick up your mat and walk.' At once the man was cured; he picked up his mat and walked" (John 5:8).*

Remember the woman who had been bleeding for twelve years, who had run out of money and doctors and all other options. She came to Jesus and said, *"If I just touch His clothes, I will get well."* Then she touched His cloak, her bleeding stopped, and Jesus said, *"Daughter, your faith has healed you. Go in peace and be freed from your suffering" (Mark 5:28, 34).*

Remember King David, who suffered much at the hands of other men—and

Below: While the once-beautiful stones from the pools are in ruins, those who have been touched by Jesus now have new bodies and new life with Him in heaven.

Left and below: The crusaders built Saint Anne's Church next to the pools of Bethesda in the 12th century over the traditional birthplace of Saint Anne (Hannah), the mother of Mary.

from his own sins, yet he wrote in the Psalms, *"Praise the LORD, O my soul, and forget not all His benefits—who forgives all your sins and heals all your diseases..." (Psalm 103:2-3).*

Remember James, the brother of Jesus, who called on those who were sick to come to Jesus in prayer for their healing: *"Is any one of you sick? He should call for the elders of the church and have them pray over them, anointing them with oil in the name of the Lord. And their prayer offered in faith will heal the sick, and the Lord will make them well" (James 5:14-15a).*

Remember Peter, who healed a crippled man who was begging for money outside the Temple by saying, *"Silver or gold I do not have, but what I have I give you. In the name of Jesus Christ of Nazareth, walk" (Acts 3:6).* Then taking the man by the hand, he helped him up to his feet, which became

strong again, and the man went walking and leaping and praising God.

Peter knew that it wasn't his own power or strength that healed the man. He knew that he was just a conduit who reached out to the One True Source of healing: Jesus.

After the healing, Peter said,

"Men of Israel, why does this surprise you? Why do you stare at us as if by our own power or godliness we had made this man walk? ... You killed the Author of Life, but God raised Him from the dead. We are witnesses of this. By faith in the name of Jesus, this man whom you see and know was made strong. It is Jesus' name and the faith that comes through Him that has given this complete healing to him, as you can all see" (Acts 3:12,16).

If you're sick, come to Jesus. If you're worn out, come to Jesus. If you've run

Above: The acoustics in Saint Anne's Church, designed for services using the Gregorian chant, are so perfect that the church is said to be, "like a musical instrument to be played by the human voice."

out of money and doctors and all other options, come to Jesus.

If you're wrestling with unhealthy thoughts, words, or deeds, come to Jesus. If you're worried sick and your emotions are shot, come to Jesus.

As Peter said,

"It is Jesus' name and the faith that comes through Him that has given this COMPLETE healing to him, as you can all see."

Do you want to get well? Come to Jesus. Let Him do His healing work in your life.

Let's pray:

Father, thank You for being a God who heals. Thank You for wanting to make us whole and complete. Thank You for designing our bodies to heal themselves when possible, for giving us wisdom to facilitate that healing power when not, and for sending us Jesus, whom we believe can heal us supernaturally at any moment—even if we'll been lame for thirty-eight years. In Jesus' name, Amen.

Lesson 23

WHAT'S GOING TO HAPPEN ON THE MOUNT OF OLIVES?

The Mount of Olives is only a short walk from the Temple Mount, and from there you can get a beautiful view of the city of Jerusalem. Jesus spent His nights there during the last week of His life, praying, sleeping, and teaching His disciples. But something else is going to happen on the Mount of Olives one day. To find out what, take a look at this short video at the link at the right.* Then read on to find out what you can do today to prepare for what's going to happen there

in the future.

So what's going to happen on the Mount of Olives? That's where Jesus will return.

Jesus often went to the Mount of Olives with His disciples when He was in Jerusalem, perhaps because it was so close to the Temple. It is just across the valley from the Temple Mount, and only a Sabbath's day's walk from the city (just over half-a mile away, the maximum distance that Jews were allowed to walk on the Sabbath). It was a convenient spot for Jesus and His disciples to retreat to after

*Watch "Mount of Olives" on the Internet at this link http://youtube.com/watch?v=s86uhi04qn0

Facing page and above left: Jerusalem, as seen from the top of the Mount of Olives, where Jesus and His disciples often went to pray and sleep. Above right: The Mount of Olives, as seen from across the valley.

teaching at the Temple during the day. The Bible says:

"Each day Jesus was teaching at the Temple, and each evening He went out to spend the night on the hill called the Mount of Olives..." (Luke 21:36-38).

But Jesus' affinity for the Mount of Olives may not have been simply because of its proximity to the Temple. The Mount of Olives is also the site where the prophet Zechariah said the Lord would appear one day, redeeming those who honored Him and destroying those who didn't:

"On that day His feet will stand on the Mount of Olives, east of Jerusalem, and the Mount of Olives will be split in two from east to west, forming a great valley, with half of the mountain moving north and half moving south" (Zechariah 14:4).

And it was from the Mount of Olives that Jesus eventually ascended into heaven after His death and resurrection here on earth. As He rose into the sky, two angels appeared to the disciples and said:

"Men of Galilee, why do you stand here looking into the sky? This same Jesus, who has been taken from you into heaven, will come back in the same way you have seen Him go into heaven." Then they returned to Jerusalem from the hill called the Mount of Olives, a Sabbath day's walk from the city (Acts 1:11-12).

So the Mount of Olives has become famous as the place where the Messiah will first appear, and over 150,000 people have been buried there on that hill—including the prophet Zechariah—in order to be on hand the moment the Messiah arrives.

But you won't have to be on the Mount of Olives to know that Jesus has come back. Jesus taught His disciples what that day would be like, the signs that would precede it, and what they could do now to prepare for it.

Listen to the words of Jesus that He spoke while still here on the earth, words that He spoke, in fact, right there on the Mount of Olives just a few days before His death:

As Jesus was sitting on the Mount of Olives, the disciples came to Him privately. "Tell us," they said, "when will this happen, and what will be the sign of Your coming and of the end of the age?"

Jesus answered: "Watch out that no one deceives you. For many will come in My name, claiming, 'I am the Christ,' and will deceive many. You will hear of wars and rumors of wars, but see to it that you are not alarmed. Such

Left: The Mount of Olives was just a Sabbath's Day's walk from the Temple Mount, where Jesus taught daily during the last week of His life.

Above: Thousands of tombs cover the Mount of Olives, including the tomb of Zechariah, who prophesied that the Messiah would one day stand there. The trees of the Garden of Gethsemane are visible, in the center, beyond the tombs.

things must happen, but the end is still to come. Nation will rise against nation, and kingdom against kingdom. There will be famines and earthquakes in various places. All these are the beginning of birth pains.

"Then you will be handed over to be persecuted and put to death, and you will be hated by all nations because of me. At that time many will turn away from the faith and will betray and hate each other, and many false prophets will appear and deceive many people. Because of the increase of wickedness, the love of most will grow cold, but he who stands firm to the end will be saved. And this gospel of the kingdom will be preached in the whole world as a testimony to all nations, and then the end will come....

"At that time if anyone says to you, 'Look, here is the Christ!' or, 'There He is!' do not believe it. For false Christs and false prophets will appear and perform great signs and miracles to deceive even the elect—if that were possible. See, I have told you ahead of time.

"So if anyone tells you, 'There He is, out in the desert,' do not go out; or, 'Here He is, in the inner rooms,' do not believe it. For as lightning that comes from the east is visible even in the west, so will be the coming of the Son of Man....

"No one knows about that day or hour, not even the angels in heaven, nor the Son, but only the Father. As it was in the days of Noah, so it will be at the coming of the Son of Man. For in the days before the flood, people were eating and

**Left:
Olives
ripen on
the Mount
of Olives.**

*drinking,
marrying
and giving
in marriage,
up to the day
Noah entered
the ark; and
they knew
nothing about
what would
happen until the
flood came and took them all away. That is how
it will be at the coming of the Son of Man. Two
men will be in the field; one will be taken and
the other left. Two women will be grinding with a
hand mill; one will be taken and the other left.*

*"Therefore keep watch, because you do not
know on what day your Lord will come. But
understand this: If the owner of the house had
known at what time of night the thief was
coming, he would have kept watch and would
not have let his house be broken into. So you also
must be ready, because the Son of Man will
come at an hour when you do not expect
Him"* (Matthew 24:1-14, 23-27, 36-44).

When I was young, I remember
hearing a lot of stories about Jesus. But
for some reason, I missed the fact that
one day He was going to come back
again! When I realized that He was really
coming back, my heart leapt! Wow! The
same Jesus who had done so many
miraculous things was going to be coming
again! What a day that would be!

But this wasn't going to be "gentle
Jesus, meek and mild" (not that He was

ever was that way when He first came
either, but that was my impression as a
child). This Jesus was going to be coming
in power and might, redeeming those who
loved Him and destroying those who
didn't.

There will be no question on that day
about whether Jesus is the Christ or not.
His re-appearance will be visible
simultaneously and instantaneously all
around the world. As Jesus said, *"For as
lightning that comes from the east is visible even
in the west, so will be the coming of the Son of
Man."* You won't have to be on the Mount
of Olives to know that Jesus is back.
You'll know it—no matter where you are
in the world!

And when that day comes, Christ
wants you to be ready. After teaching His
disciples to look for the signs of His
coming, Jesus then told three parables,
stories that describe what will happen to
those who are prepared for His return,
and what will happen to those who aren't.
If you haven't read them lately, you might
want to read them again this week. You
can find them in Matthew chapter 25: the
parables about the ten virgins, the talents,
and the sheep and the goats.

Jesus summarized them like this:

*"Who then is the faithful and wise servant,
whom the master has put in charge of the
servants in his household to give them their food
at the proper time? It will be good for that
servant whose master finds him doing so when he
returns. I tell you the truth, he will put him in
charge of all his possessions. But suppose that
servant is wicked and says to himself, 'My
master is staying away a long time,' and he then
begins to beat his fellow servants and to eat and
drink with drunkards. The master of that
servant will come on a day when he does not*

expect him and at an hour he is not aware of. He will cut him to pieces and assign him a place with the hypocrites, where there will be weeping and gnashing of teeth" (Matthew 24:45-51).

When Jesus returns, He wants to find you with your hearts firmly committed to Him, ready and eagerly desiring His coming, as a bride eagerly desires the coming of her groom.

He wants to find you using the talents He has given you, not squandering away the resources and abilities He has given you, but using them to make a good return on His investment.

He wants to find you doing the things that He's called all of us to do, both spiritually and physically: giving food to the hungry, drink to the thirsty, inviting in strangers, clothing the naked, caring for the sick, and visiting those in prison.

I want to encourage you today to get ready for His return. If your heart's not fully committed to Jesus, make that commitment today. If you know someone whose heart's not fully committed to Jesus, send this message to them and encourage them to make that commitment today.

And if your heart *is* fully committed to Jesus, get ready for His return! Look forward to it! Look forward to the day when He stands again on the Mount of Olives, in the fullness of His glory, coming back to take you to be with Him forever! Fill your hearts with faith today, make a good return on the gifts He has given you, and serve one another wholeheartedly. Remember, as Jesus said, *"...he who stands firm to the end will be saved" (Matthew 24:13).*

Let's pray:

Father, thank You for the reminder that Jesus is coming back again, and that He will one day take us to be with Him forever. Lord, fill our hearts with faith again today, faith that Jesus will indeed come back for us, and faith that will inspire us to keep doing Your work here on earth right up until that day comes. We put our faith, hope and trust in You again today. In Jesus' name, Amen.

Right: The Mount of Olives, where Jesus will first stand when He returns.

Lesson 24

WHAT HAPPENED AT THE GARDEN OF GETHSEMANE?

The Garden of Gethsemane is made up of a grove of olive trees found at the foot of the Mount of Olives. The word "gethsemane" means "oil press," and this garden likely served as the location of an ancient olive press, a device used to squeeze the oil out of olives. But another kind of pressing took place on the night before Jesus died. It was, perhaps, His most difficult trial on earth. To find out what happened that night, and how He faced it, take a look at this short video at the link below.* Then read on to find out how God can give you the strength to pass the trials you face as well.

So what happened at the Garden of Gethsemane? This is where Jesus went to pray the night He was betrayed.

If you remember the story, the trial He faced that night was so difficult that He told His disciples He was *overwhelmed with sorrow to the point of death" (Mark 14:34a)*. When Jesus tried to get His disciples to stay awake with Him during the night, they couldn't do it. This was a trial He was going

*Watch "Garden of Gethsemane" on the Internet at this link http://youtube.com/watch?v=LWPY2lu2iAo

Facing page and above left: The Garden of Gethsemane, located on the side of the Mount of Olives, still contains ancient olive trees over a thousand years old. Above right: The Garden as seen from above.

Above: The Church of all Nations was built in the 1920's at the Garden of Gethsemane, over a site where churches have stood since the 4th century.

to have to face without them.

But He didn't have to face it alone. He faced it together with God His Father in prayer. The words Jesus prayed that night are an encouragement to me, as they have been to people for thousands of years, people who have faced trials of many kinds. Jesus said:

"My Father, if it is possible, may this cup be taken from Me. Yet not as I will, but as You will" (Matthew 25:42).

You may have heard these words so many times that they've lost their freshness, but I'd like to remind you today of the power contained within them. They are words that can bring you peace and restore life to your soul once again no matter what kind of situation you might be facing.

First, know that when you face a

trial of any kind, you're not facing it alone. When you get to that point where you feel so alone that even your closest friends seem unable to walk with you through it any further, know that God is still there to walk through it with you.

When Jesus prayed that night, He went to His Father not just once or twice, but three times. Before each time of prayer, He asked His disciples to stay awake and keep watch for Him. But the fact that they couldn't do it didn't mean that His friends didn't love Him, or that they didn't want to help Him. They wanted to do whatever He asked, but in the end they simply couldn't do it. Jesus knew their

Right: Glittering mosaics line the walls within the church.

hearts were still with Him nonetheless, and He said:

"The spirit is willing, but the body is weak" *(Matthew 26:41).*

But even though Jesus' disciples fell asleep, God never did. The Bible says that God never slumbers nor sleeps (see Psalm 121:4). Each time Jesus found the disciples sleeping, He returned to God in prayer.

Second, know that it's not unspiritual to plead with God for that which you think is best. Three times, Jesus said:

"My Father, if it is possible, may this cup be taken from Me."

Jesus didn't want to face what lay ahead of Him. He pleaded with God to take it away, to change His course, or to show Him another path. It wasn't that Jesus wanted to disobey His Father's will, but neither did He hide the fact that He'd rather do it another way if possible!

The anguish that Jesus faced that night was intense, so intense that Luke says:

"His sweat was like drops of blood falling to the ground" *(Luke 22:44).*

The pressure of it all, the squeezing that He felt must have been nearly unbearable. The pain and twisting he felt may have been mirrored in the gnarled and twisted olive trees found in the

Right: Tall exterior doors open up to the highly decorated interior doors of the church, depicting the olive trees outside.

Above: The ancient olive trees are still producing fruit today at Gethsemane, the Greek word for "oil press."

was a Christian who suffered much during her lifetime in France in the 1700's. Yet through it all she was able to find the peace of God by surrendering her will to God's. She wrote: *"All your concerns go into the hand of God. You forget yourself, and from that moment on you think only of Him. By continuing to do this over a long period of time, your heart will remain unattached; your heart will be free and at peace! How do you practice abandonment? You practice it daily, hourly and by the moment. Abandonment is practiced by continually losing your own will in the will of God—by plunging your will into the depths of His will, there to be lost forever!"* (Madame Guyon, *Experiencing the Depths of Jesus Christ*).

Garden of Gethsemane itself, some of which are over 1,000 years old—and some could have even been alive at the time of Christ, as olives tree can, remarkably, live several *thousand* years.

Jesus knew that the pain ahead could be severe, and He didn't hesitate to pray that His Father would make another way. If it wasn't "unspiritual" for Jesus to pray this way, then I wouldn't think it would be unspiritual for you to ask for it either.

But third, know that whatever happens in the end, you can trust God to work all things for good, when you truly commit your will to His. Madame Guyon

While it is important to remember that God has given us free will—the will or desire do that which we want—it's also important to remember that God has a will, too. While God wants to give you the desires of your heart, He also has desires on *His* heart, desires which often go way beyond ours!

I am a firm believer that God wants to bless you, to prosper you, and to make you healthy and wealthy and wise. The Scriptures are full of stories of how God has come through for His people, blessing them with healing and prosperity, both physically and spiritually, and pouring out His wisdom upon them. But I am also a firm believer that God's blessings can often exceed our own, but sometimes we can only see them as blessings when we look at them through eyes of faith.

I once heard a long-time and well-respected Christian leader say that when he looked back on his life, it turned out that the times he thought were his mountaintop turned out to be the valleys, and the times he thought he was going through the valleys turned out to be the mountaintops. God has a way of bringing good from every situation, when we trust Him to do His will in all things.

Know that God wants to bless you, that He wants to bless others through you, and that you can trust Him in all things, at all times, to work His will, in His ways. Know that when He calls you to face your own Garden of Gethsemane, you won't face it alone. You'll be in good company, the likes of which

includes Jesus Christ Himself, the One who trusted His Father inherently and said with His whole heart:

"My Father, if it is possible, may this cup be taken from Me. Yet not as I will, but as You will."

I pray that you'll be able to do the same.

Let's pray:

Father, thank You for never leaving us alone, thank You for giving us our own free will, and thank You for giving us the confidence that Your will always is always better than our own. Help us to come to You with complete abandonment so that we can experience the fullness of Your peace, Your joy, and Your life that will come to us when we do. In Jesus' name, Amen.

Right: The prayers that Jesus said in the Garden show us that we can trust God with the outcome of all things, when we entrust it into His hands.

WHAT HAPPENED AT THE HOUSE OF CAIAPHAS?

Caiaphas was the high priest at the time when Jesus was betrayed, and it was to Caiaphas' house that Jesus was brought and accused of blasphemy against God. To see the dungeon of this house, and the adjoining pit where prisoners were lowered into by a rope to prevent them from escaping, take a look at this short video at the link at the right.* Then read on to find out what else happened that night at Caiaphas' house, and how God can restore, redeem, and forgive you, too, if you've ever felt that you've done something against Him.

So what happened at the House of Caiaphas? That's where Peter denied Jesus three times.

After Jesus was betrayed by Judas in the Garden of Gethsemane, the guards brought Jesus to the house of Caiaphas, the high priest. Jesus was taken inside and tried for blasphemy, while Peter waited in the courtyard outside to find out what was going to happen.

*Watch "House of Caiaphas" on the Internet at this link http://youtube.com/ watch?v=52ULi85cyAg

Facing page: The church that was built over the House of Caiaphas, where Peter denied Christ three times (note the golden rooster). Above: Beautifully decorated doors, and the dark pit inside and below.

But while Peter was waiting, some people in the crowd recognized him as having been with Jesus. Apparently overcome by fear, Peter denied that he even knew Jesus, not just once or twice, but three times. The Bible says:

Now Peter was sitting out in the courtyard, and a servant girl came to him. "You also were with Jesus of Galilee" she said.

But he denied it before them all. "I don't know what you're talking about," he said.

Then he went out to the gateway, where another girl saw him and said to the people there, "This fellow was with Jesus of Nazareth."

He denied it again, with an oath: "I don't know the man!"

After a little while, those standing there went up to Peter and said, "Surely you are one of them, for your accent gives you away."

Then he began to call down curses on himself and he swore to them, "I don't know the man!" (Matthew 26:69-74).

This was, perhaps, the worst night in Jesus' life. But it was also probably the worst night in Peter's life as well. When Peter realized what he had done, the Bible says, *"he went outside and wept bitterly."*

Looking back on the situation, we can forgive Peter for what he did that night—for under the same circumstances, who knows what any of us might have done? And yet I think it would have been harder for Peter to forgive himself. For it was Peter who, just a few hours earlier, at the Passover dinner, said to Jesus:

"Even if all fall away on account of You, I never will.... Even if I have to die with You, I will never disown You" (Matthew 26: 33, 35).

But Jesus knew what Peter was going to do, and mercifully He told Peter ahead of time, speaking

Left: An ornamental lamp now leads the way down into the dark pit where Christ was held and beaten on the night He was betrayed by the Jewish guards.

words of restoration to Peter even before he sinned. What a gracious Friend and Lord.

Here's what Jesus said to Peter, also known as Simon, earlier in the night:

"Simon, Simon, Satan has asked to sift you as wheat. But I have prayed for you, Simon, that your faith may not fail. And when you have turned back, strengthen your brothers" (Luke 22:31, 32).

Jesus knew that all the disciples would fall away from Him that night, including Peter. But Jesus came to Peter specifically to let him know that He was praying for Him that his faith wouldn't fail. Then He encouraged Peter to strengthen his brothers when he did turn back.

A church has now been built over the House of Caiaphas. It has been named in honor of Saint Peter and is called "The Church of Saint Peter in Gallicantu"—although I'm not sure that Peter would prefer the honor, since "gallicantu" means "cock-crow" in Latin, a reminder of the words Jesus spoke to Peter earlier that night:

"I tell you the truth, this very night, before the rooster crows, you will disown me three times" (Matthew 26:34).

But then again, Peter may truly appreciate the honor, for even though it showed his weakness, it also showed Christ's strength: to restore those who have fallen far, far from their faith. Jesus' restoration of Peter continued a short time later on the beach at the Sea of Galilee when, after Jesus died and rose again from the dead, He appeared yet again to the disciples.

Above: A statue of Christ, bound by those who didn't believe He was the Christ.

Taking Peter aside for a very personal conversation, Jesus asked Peter three times if Peter loved Him. The Bible says:

When they had finished eating, Jesus said to Simon Peter, "Simon son of John, do you truly love me more than these?"

"Yes, Lord," he said, "You know that I love You."

Jesus said, "Feed My lambs."

Again Jesus said, "Simon son of John, do you truly love me?"

He answered, "Yes, Lord, You know that I love You."

Jesus said, "Take care of My sheep."

The third time He said to him, "Simon son of John, do you love me?"

Above: Outside the Church of Saint Peter in Gallicantu, looking toward the Mount of Olives.

Peter was hurt because Jesus asked him the third time, "Do you love me?" He said, "Lord, You know all things; You know that I love You."

Jesus said, "Feed My sheep" (John 21:15-17).

It's as if Jesus was giving Peter a chance to redeem himself, saying that He loved Jesus three times, perhaps to counteract the three times had Peter denied Him. And the restoration took hold, for Peter went on to feed Jesus' sheep in a powerful way, leading the church in Jerusalem for the rest of his life, proclaiming Jesus' name everywhere he went, and facing threats of death without fear from those who opposed his message.

Perhaps you've felt like Peter before on the night that he denied Jesus. Perhaps you've felt you've done something so horrible, at least in your mind, that you believe Jesus could never forgive you. Maybe you've cheated or lied or stolen. Maybe you've had an affair or betrayed your family or friends. Maybe you've denied Christ in ways that only you and He could fully comprehend. If so, you might wonder if Jesus could ever forgive you, restore you, and use you ever again.

If that's the case, I want to remind you today that Jesus knew about Peter's sins even before he committed them. And He knows about yours and mine. And still, He was willing to die for Peter and you and me, even while we were still involved in our sins. That's the way that the Bible says God demonstrates His love for us:

"But God demonstrates His own love for us in this: While we were still sinners, Christ died for us" (Romans 5:8).

If you're wrestling with the idea of forgiveness, and whether or not God can or will forgive you of your sins, I pray today that God will show you His unsurpassing love. I pray that these words from the Bible will wash over you. And I pray that you'll know that if you ask God for forgiveness, and put your faith in Christ, that He will indeed forgive you, removing your sins from you as far as the east is from the west, and remembering them no more.

As the Bible says:

"If we confess our sins, He is faithful and just and will forgive us our sins and purify us from all unrighteousness" (1 John 1:9).

"...as far as the east is from the west, so far has He removed our transgressions from us" (Psalm 103:12).

"For I will forgive their wickedness and will remember their sins no more" (Hebrews 8:12).

While the House of Caiaphas may stand as a reminder of Peter's worst possible sin in his life, it also stands as a beacon of hope for all those need a reminder that Christ can restore, redeem, and forgive them, too.

Let's pray:

Father, thank You for making a way for us to come back to You when we've sinned. Give us the boldness to come back to You again today, leaving our past behind, and walking ahead in the calling that You have on each one of our lives. In Jesus' name, Amen.

Below: The elaborately decorated, domed ceiling of Saint Peter in Gallicantu reminds us of the glory that came out of the suffering that took place here.

Lesson 26

WHAT HAPPENED ON THE VIA DOLOROSA?

The Via Dolorosa is a path that winds its way through the streets of Jerusalem, and upon which millions have walked over the years. Why? Because another Man walked this path one day—the most painful day of His life. To see what the path looks like today, and find out why it's called the Via Dolorosa, take a look at this short video at the link at the right.* Then read on to find out how God can give you the strength to get through the painful days in your life as well.

So what happened on the Via Dolorosa? That's the path that Jesus took as He carried His cross to His crucifixion.

The words "via dolorosa" are Latin for "the way of suffering." And while the Via Dolorosa is a path that many people have taken over the years, not many people ever really want to take the "way of suffering" in life. Suffering goes against human nature, and pain is usually a God-given indicator to let you know that something is wrong and needs to be fixed.

But there are times when God may call you to take a path that leads

*Watch "Via Dolorosa" on the Internet at this link http://youtube.com/watch?v=XvqBqa5Id8I

Facing page: The Via Dolorosa means the "way of suffering," the path that Christ took to His execution. Above: Signs mark the traditional route, and fresh bread is wheeled through the streets to the market.

"Let us fix our eyes on Jesus, the Author and Perfecter of our faith, who for the joy set before Him endured the cross, scorning its shame, and sat down at the right hand of the throne of God. Consider Him who endured such opposition from sinful men, so that you will not grow weary and lose heart" (Hebrews 12:2-3).

It was for the joy set before Jesus that He was able to endure the cross. If there was any other way, Jesus would have taken it. He said as much in the Garden of Gethsemane the night before He had to walk down the Via Dolorosa. He prayed:

"My Father, if it is possible, may this cup be taken from Me. Yet not as I will, but as You will" (Matthew 25:42).

While none of us wants to enter into pain and suffering voluntarily—not even Jesus—He showed us how to do it when the time comes for us to enter into it.

He kept His eyes on the prize. When the guards came to take Him away, He went. When they asked Him to carry His cross, He carried it. And when He could carry it no longer by Himself, God sent someone else to carry it for Him:

"Carrying His own cross, He went out to the place of the Skull (which in Aramaic is called Golgotha)" (John 19:17). *"As they were*

directly into pain—not because He wants you to suffer, but because He has something better in mind for you on the other side of the pain.

Examples abound:

- Like a pregnant woman who has to endure nine months of labor and the pain of childbirth in order to experience the joy of holding her newborn baby in her arms,

- Or like a teenage girl who has to break up with her boyfriend because she wants to remain pure for her future husband,

- Or like a man with a gash in his arm who has to endure the cleansing and stitching of the wound so that his flesh can eventually be healed.

Jesus showed us the key to making it through times of suffering like these: by keeping your eyes on the prize. As the Bible says:

Right: Station 5 marks the place where Simon of Cyrene picked up the cross of Jesus and carried it for Him.

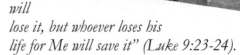

going out, they met a man from Cyrene, named Simon, and they forced him to carry the cross" (Matthew 27:32).

You can still see the place marked on the Via Dolorosa where Simon of Cyrene may have taken up Jesus' cross for Him. It's one of fourteen "stations of the cross" that are marked out along the path, stations that are replicated in many churches throughout the world. If people want to remember all that Jesus did for them in those last few hours of His life, they can walk around the perimeter of the church and stop to meditate at any of these fourteen stations, just as they can on the real Via Dolorosa in Jerusalem.

Walking along the Via Dolorosa is a reminder not only of the suffering that Jesus endured for us, but also of the suffering that He sometimes calls us to endure for Him. As Jesus told His disciples:

"If anyone would come after Me, he must deny himself and take up his cross daily and follow Me. For whoever wants to save his life

will lose it, but whoever loses his life for Me will save it" (Luke 9:23-24).

Although no one ever wants to suffer, Jesus' words are a reminder that some things are worth suffering for, that there is a prize awaiting those who endure it to the end, and that God wants you to have it.

Right: Cats roam along the Via Dolorosa early in the morning before the shops open and the crowds arrive all along the street.

The best way to go through suffering is to make sure you set your eyes on the prize. But it's also important to make sure you're setting your eyes on the right prize. There's nothing worse than enduring pain and suffering, only to find that what you've been waiting for all along has been lost in the process.

If your hope is set on having the perfect family, and then something happens to destroy that perfection, you'll be disappointed. If you're working your hardest to get a promotion, then the promotion doesn't come, you'll be upset. If you give up your dreams in order to help someone else fulfill theirs, but then they blow it and waste all that you've given up for them, you might wonder if it was worth it.

Sometimes these disappointments come because our eyes weren't on the right prize in the first place. Even Peter, who may have expected Jesus to ride into Jerusalem, overthrow the Romans and setup His new kingdom, was willing to die for Jesus as He ascended to His throne. But when Peter found out that Jesus had been arrested, and was likely going to be sentenced to death, his disappointment was evident. Instead of standing up for Jesus anymore, he denied that he even knew him. Perhaps it was because his eyes were on the wrong prize for the moment.

But God honored Peter still, just like He honors all those who love Him and who are called according to His purpose. He eventually showed Peter that Jesus reigned in a kingdom whose authority went beyond Jerusalem, beyond the Romans, and extended over the entire earth. It was better than Peter could have ever expected. We're told that Peter eventually did give up his life for Jesus, being crucified on a cross upside-down. But this time he had his eyes on the right prize, and he was willing to walk down the path of suffering to get it.

As much as God wants to relieve you of much of the suffering you'll face in life, He also wants you to

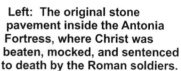

Left: The original stone pavement inside the Antonia Fortress, where Christ was beaten, mocked, and sentenced to death by the Roman soldiers.

Above: The Via Dolorosa is a reminder to us that we need to keep our "eyes on the prize" as we walk through life, just as Jesus did.

know that some things are achieved only by going through it.

God wants you to trust Him. He wants you to trust that He is able to do *"immeasurably more than all we could ask or imagine" (Ephesians 3:20a).* Keep your eyes on the prize, and if you can't see the prize, then keep your eyes on Jesus. In the end, it will all be worth it.

Let's pray:

Father, thank You for Jesus' example, that we can follow in His steps. Help us to trust that the suffering in our life is worth it, when we entrust our lives completely to You. Help us to take up our cross daily and be willing to die for you, so that we can find the life that You've wanted us to have all along. In Jesus' name, Amen.

Lesson 27

WHAT HAPPENED AT GOLGOTHA?

Golgotha means "the place of the skull." It's not a very happy-sounding name, and what took place here was most likely even more gruesome than the name suggests. But on the other hand, what took place here at Golgotha is what has made it the holiest site in all of Christendom. To find out what happened here, and why it matters to so many people, take a look at this short video at the link at the right.* Then read on to find out how God can use the sadness of what

happened at Golgotha to bring incredible joy to your life today.

So what happened at Golgotha? That's where Jesus died, was buried, and rose again again from the dead.

When Jesus was arrested and sentenced to death, He and those who were to be executed with Him walked through the streets of Jerusalem, carrying their crosses when they could, and having others carry their crosses for them when they couldn't. Eventually they came to the execution site. The Bible says:

*Watch "Golgotha" on the Internet at this link http://youtube.com/watch?v=Q_ndvxnVXJ0

Facing page: The altar in the Church of the Holy Sepulchre marks the spot where the cross of Christ once stood. Above left: The cross and candles above the altar, and the entrance to the church.

167

Above: An archway leads into the plaza in front of the Church of the Holy Seuplchre. "Sepulchre" means tomb.

They came to a place called Golgotha (which means The Place of the Skull). There they offered Jesus wine to drink, mixed with gall; but after tasting it, He refused to drink it. When they had crucified Him, they divided up His clothes by casting lots. And sitting down, they kept watch over Him there (Matthew 26:33-36).

Golgotha was undoubtedly a horrific place, just outside the walls of the city at the time of Christ. It seems to have gotten its name either because of all the crucifixions that took place there, or because the hill itself actually resembled a skull. Either way, the hill called Golgotha was a picture of death.

But the day that Christ died there, something changed. When Christ died on the cross, Golgotha became a picture of life, filled with the beauty of sacrificial love.

There's a song that explains how Golgotha—and the cross of Christ— could come to represent such an unusual mixture of death and life. George Bennard said it this way in his song, *The Old Rugged Cross:*

On a hill far away stood an old rugged cross, the emblem of suffering and shame; and I love that old cross where the dearest and best for a world of lost sinners was slain.
In that old rugged cross, stained with blood so divine, a wondrous beauty I see, for 'twas on that old cross Jesus suffered and died, to pardon and sanctify me.

This is why crosses are so prevalent in jewelry, churches, and other holy places. It's not because Christians have some perverse fascination with death, like wearing little guillotines around their necks on a chain. Jesus didn't express His love to us by dying on a guillotine. He expressed it by dying on a cross. And it's the love that Christ expressed for us when He died on the cross that we celebrate as Christians, and that's why we make so much of His cross.

It is both an "emblem of suffering and shame," and also a "wondrous beauty" to behold, all at the same time.

There are two spots in Jerusalem that are considered potential locations of Christ's crucifixion. One is the Garden Tomb, which was discovered in 1848 and which I highlighted in the introduction of this book. The other is the Church of the Holy Sepulchre ("sepulchre" means "tomb" in Latin), and has been the traditional site of the crucifixion since the 1st and 2nd century. Today I'd like to focus on the the Church of the Holy Sepulchre.

For those interested, the church itself was first built and dedicated in 335 A.D. by Helena, the mother of Constantine, after she had been shown this site by the believers in Jerusalem at that time. The church has undergone many changes over the years, but the location has remained the same.

When I walked into the Church of the Holy Sepulchre for the first time, and up the stairs to the right that led to the top of the small hill called Golgotha over which the church was built, I was overcome with emotion. It wasn't because of anything I saw there—for it was filled with candles and tourists and objects that glittered with gold. I was overcome with emotion because of what had happened there.

I dropped to my knees. I thanked God for all He had done for me there. And I cried.

I knew that Jesus wasn't the One who should have died on the cross that day. He was totally innocent. It should have been me. It was me who had sinned, and it was me who should have had to pay the price for those sins. But Jesus did it for me, of His own free will, as a demonstration of His love for me.

Below: Light from above the dome streams down onto the traditional spot where Jesus was lain in the tomb and rose from the dead.

He could have called twelve legions of angels to rescue Him if He had wanted, as He told Peter in the Garden of Gethsemane (see Matthew 26:53). But He didn't.

The fact that Jesus stepped in to pay for my sins with His life has been, and still is, the greatest expression of love I have ever felt in my life. While others have loved me dearly, like my family and friends, Jesus is the only one who could have stepped in and did for me what He did: fully forgiving me of my sins.

When I got back up from my knees, I walked downstairs again and to the other side of the massive church, to the spot where they believe Jesus was buried in a tomb nearby. The walls and ceiling of the tomb have been destroyed over the years, as the church has changed hands and been

Below: A slab of marble, between the crucifixion site and the tomb, that marks where Joseph and Nicodemus may have anointed Jesus' body and wrapped it for burial.

ransacked many times since then. Only a plain slab of rock remains of the place where they believe He was lain, and that is housed in a small chapel under the great dome of the church.

While there's little to see there, of course, for neither Christ nor much of the tomb are there, the site is vivid enough in the memories of those who are familiar with the story to recreate in their minds the scene of what happened there. As it says in the Bible:

"Later, Joseph of Arimathea asked Pilate for the body of Jesus. Now Joseph was a disciple of Jesus, but secretly because he feared the Jews. With Pilate's permission, he came and took the body away. He was accompanied by Nicodemus, the man who earlier had visited Jesus at night. Nicodemus brought a mixture of myrrh and aloes, about seventy-five pounds. Taking Jesus' body, the two of them wrapped it, with the spices, in strips of linen. This was in accordance with Jewish burial customs. At the place where Jesus was crucified, there was a garden, and in the garden a new tomb, in which no one had ever been laid. Because it was the Jewish day of Preparation and since the tomb was nearby, they laid Jesus there." (John 19:38-42).

And then, a few days later:

After the Sabbath, at dawn on the first day of the week, Mary Magdalene and the other Mary went to look at the tomb.

There was a violent earthquake, for an angel of the Lord came down from heaven and, going to the tomb, rolled back the stone and sat on it. His appearance was like lightning, and his clothes were white as snow. The guards were so afraid of him that they shook and became like dead men.

The angel said to the women, "Do not be afraid, for I know that you are looking for Jesus, who was crucified. He is not here; He has risen, just as He said. Come and see the place where He lay. Then go quickly and tell His disciples: 'He has risen from the dead and is going ahead of you into Galilee. There you will see Him.' Now I have told you" (Matthew 28:1-7).

So you can see why this place has become such a sacred spot to those who claim Jesus as their Lord. While the ravages of time, battles, earthquakes, and fires have taken their toll on the Church of the Holy Sepulchre, the events that made this place so holy are no less compelling today than they were when they first took place.

Above: Constantine's magnificent church has been destroyed and rebuilt many times since 335 A.D.—but no amount of architecture or ornamentation could ever express what Christ has done for us.

It is not the church itself that has brought millions of people like me here to visit it. It is the realization that what happened here was real, and that God really did love us so much that He sent His one and only Son to die for us so that we could put our faith in Him and live forever.

As incredible it is to be able to be able to go to Jerusalem and touch the ground where Jesus died and rose again, if there was one thing that I could encourage you to do in your lifetime, it wouldn't be to go to Jerusalem. It would be to go to Jesus, to put your faith in Him who died on the cross for your sins, rose again from the dead, and who now calls you to live your life for Him, following Him here on earth and on into heaven.

If there's sin in your life, drop it now at the foot of His cross. If you're involved in lying or stealing, gossiping or cheating, pre-marital or extra-marital or any other kind of sinful sex, turn away from it today and turn back again. If you're burying your gifts in the sand, saving them for no one and nothing in particular, dig them out and put them to work for the kingdom of God. You'll be blessed when you do and so will those around you.

Most of all, you'll be able to express your love back to Christ , the One who expressed His love for you—and for all to see—there on the hill called Golgotha.

Let's pray:

Father, thank You for sending Jesus to die for our sins, and for giving us the chance to be forgiven when we put our faith in Him. Thank You for filling us with Your Holy Spirit, to enable us to do the work here on earth that You've called us to do. And thank You for promising to take us to be with You in heaven when our life on earth is over, where we can live with You forever. In Jesus' name, Amen.

WHAT HAPPENED AT
THE UPPER ROOM?

The Upper Room is perhaps best known as the location of Jesus' last supper with His disciples. But something else happened in the Upper Room just fifty days after Jesus rose from the dead, something Jesus told them to expect and to wait for. To find out what happened, take a look at this short video at the link at the right.* Then read on to find out what God wants you to do with all the things that you've learned about Him!

So what happened at the Upper Room? That's where the Holy Spirit came at Pentecost. God's Spirit flowed into the people gathered there, causing them to praise God in all kinds of languages. As a result of this outpouring of the Holy Spirit, over 3,000 people put their faith in Christ.

It wasn't something that Peter and the other disciples could have done on their own, but God used their voices to reach out to people, who came from all over the world at the time, so that they could hear all that Christ had done for them.

After Jesus rose from the dead, He appeared again to the disciples and over five hundred others throughout Jerusalem for

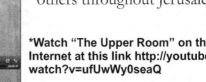
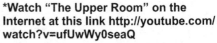

*Watch "The Upper Room" on the Internet at this link http://youtube.com/watch?v=ufUwWy0seaQ

Facing page and above: The Upper Room displays a variety of architecture and styles, having changed hands many times throughout its 2,000 year history.

a period of forty days. On one of these occasions, Jesus said:

"Do not leave Jerusalem, but wait for the gift My Father promised, which you have heard Me speak about. For John baptized with water, but in a few days you will be baptized with the Holy Spirit. ... You will receive power when the Holy Spirit comes on you; and you will be My witnesses in Jerusalem, and in all Judea and Samaria, and to the ends of the earth" (Acts 1:4-5, 8).

So when Jesus went up into heaven, the disciples went back to the room where they were staying. Luke called it an "upper room" (Acts 1:13, KJV), just as he had done when describing the place where they had eaten their last supper (see Luke 22:12). It was here, apparently, that:

"They all joined together constantly in prayer, along with the women and Mary the mother of Jesus, and with His brothers" (Acts 1:14).

About ten days later, on the fiftieth day since Jesus rose from the dead (and the day of Pentecost, which comes from the Greek word for "fifty"), God sent His Holy Spirit, just as Jesus promised:

"When the day of Pentecost came, they were all together in

one place. Suddenly a sound like the blowing of a violent wind came from heaven and filled the whole house where they were sitting. They saw what seemed to be tongues of fire that separated and came to rest on each of them. All of them were filled with the Holy Spirit and began to speak in other tongues as the Spirit enabled them" (Acts 2:1).*

As they spoke, others began to hear them praising God in their own languages, people from all different parts of the world who had come to Jerusalem for the festivals. Some were amazed, but others thought they had just been drinking too much wine.

Peter, who had denied Jesus just a few weeks earlier, stood up with the other disciples, and spoke to the crowd:

"Fellow Jews and all of you who live in Jerusalem, let me explain this to you; listen carefully to what I say. These men are not drunk, as you suppose. It's only nine in the morning!" (Acts 2:14-15).

He went on to say that this was the work of the Holy Spirit, whom the prophet Joel said would be poured out on the people in the last days.

Peter spoke about Jesus and how, even though Jesus had done many signs and wonders and miracles in their presence, they still handed Him over to be crucified. After telling them at length from the Scriptures who Jesus was and what they had done to Him, they were all cut to the heart. They cried out to Peter and the other apostles:

"Brothers, what shall we do?"

Peter replied, "Repent and be baptized, every one of you, in the name of Jesus

Left: The Upper Room is located above King David's tomb, which lies beneath this cloth.

Left and above: A mezuzah hangs on the doorframe outside David's Tomb, as it does outside most Jewish homes and buildings. The mezuzah is actually a piece of paper, tucked inside a holder, with the words of the "Shema Yisrael" written upon it from Deuteronomy 6, starting with: "Hear, O Israel: The Lord our God, the Lord is one..."

Christ for the forgiveness of your sins. And you will receive the gift of the Holy Spirit. The promise is for you and your children and for all who are far off—for all whom the Lord our God will call."

With many other words he warned them; and he pleaded with them, "Save yourselves from this corrupt generation." Those who accepted his message were baptized, and about three thousand were added to their number that day (Acts 2:37-41).

It's a powerful story on many fronts:

• What Jesus said would happen did happen,

• The same Peter who denied Jesus earlier now proclaimed His name to thousands,

• The Spirit came in a way that was both astounding and perplexing to those who saw it,

• About 3,000 put their faith in Christ and were baptized in a single day.

And that was just the beginning. In the days that followed, the disciples continued to do more wonders and miraculous signs:

"And the Lord added to their number daily those who were being saved" (Acts 2:47b).

Soon, those who followed Christ were taking the gospel beyond Jerusalem to Judea and Samaria and to the ends of the earth, just as Jesus said they would.

What does this all mean to you? Well, if you've never put your faith in Christ, do it today, just like those who heard the message on the day of Pentecost did! And if you've already put your faith in Christ, tell others about it so they can put their faith in Christ, too!

When we were in Israel, we had a local Israeli guide who took us from place to

175

Above: The Upper Room still inspires people ("instills" them with His "spirit") to spread the good news of Christ throughout the world.

place and taught us many things about the places that we were seeing. On the final day, our guide said, "Today, my job is finished. Tomorrow, yours begins. Your job is to go back and tell others what you have learned."

Isn't that the way God loves to work? God could, if He wanted to, put some kind of cosmic loud speakers in the sky, telling everyone that He exists, that He loves them, and that He wants them to leave their sins and come back into a relationship with Him. (And in many ways, He has already done this—see Psalm 19:1-4 or Romans 1:18-20.)

But God's preferred method is to use the voices of people—yours and mine—

to tell others about His love for them, and to share with them everything they have heard and learned and known to be true.

As we near the end of this devotional tour of Israel, I wanted to remind you of why God wanted to teach you all that you've learned about Him so far. First of all, it's for you, so that You will know Him better and fall in love with Him more deeply. But secondly, it's for you to share with others, so they may know Him better and fall in love with Him more deeply, too.

As our Israeli guide said to us, I want to say to you: "Today, my job ends. Tomorrow, yours begins!" If you're not sure how to share what you've learned with others, here are a few ideas.

1) Ask God to pour out His Holy Spirit upon you in ways that you may have never known before, so that You can proclaim His name to those around you. How can this help? The same way it helped Peter, who went from being afraid to even tell anyone that He knew Christ to being able to proclaim His name before thousands.

2) Study your Bible deeply, every day, so that you may know with confidence the truth of what you believe. Find a good study Bible, with footnotes and commentary if possible, to help you grow in the knowledge of all that God wants to say to you. Remember, too, that it's not just a time to study, but a time to spend with the One who created you, who knows you best, and who loves you more than anyone else in the world.

3) Start sharing what you've learned so far about Christ. Whether it's sharing a simple comment or two on someone's Facebook page about God's love for

them, or taking an evangelism class at a local church so that you can sharpen what and how you share with others, look for and take the opportunities God gives you to let others know about your own relationship with Him so that they can grow in *their* relationship with Him.

4) Share the messages in this book with others! Point them to our website at www.theranch.org, send them links to the YouTube videos, give them copies of this book! These resources were created to help bring the Bible to life for as many as people as possible.

While I loved going to Israel so that I could learn more about Christ for myself, I also loved going to Israel so that I could share more about Christ with others. My prayer is that you will do the same.

Whether you go to Israel in person, or experience it through the Bible and books like these, I pray that you will be filled with God's Holy Spirit to the point of overflowing, so that whatever God pours out onto you will be flow out onto to others, bringing joy and life to you, to them, and to the God who created us all.

Let's pray:

Father, thank You for pouring out Your Holy Spirit on those who gathered together for prayer in Jerusalem. We pray that You will pour out Your Holy Spirit on us again today so that we may lead others into a deeper relationship with You as well. Give us the wisdom to do it, the courage to do it, and the way to do it. Then help us take the steps of faith we need to take to proclaim Your name throughout the earth. In Jesus' name, Amen.

Below: Part of being a follower of Christ means taking what you've learned from Him and sharing it with others.

מנורת הזהב Golden Menorah

MAKING A CHANCE

Thanks for joining us on this devotional tour of the Holy Land. To see a few highlights of our trip together, take a look at this short video at the link at the right, as our worship leaders from the trip, Lucas Elder and Gary Marini, lead us in a closing song.* Then read on to hear a touching story of God's faithfulness to those who put their faith in Him.

I was telling a group one time that they should try to go to Israel if they ever got a chance. My son Lucas added: "Don't just wait till you get a chance. Make a chance! Do whatever you can do to get there. It's worth it!" He's right.

So I'd like to tell you just one more story as we close, a story about "making a chance." While I usually try to shorten stories to make them as concise as possible, I think this one is best told with all the details in tact. I believe God has several things He might want to speak to you through this story, so I pray that you'll be blessed as you read it.

As we began talking about going on this trip to Israel, a woman from Malawi named Esther had written to me, saying that she wondered if I thought God would ever make a way for her to visit Israel someday. She said she simply began crying every time she read the word "Israel" in some of the devotionals I had

*Watch "Thanks for joining us!" on the Internet at this link http://youtube.com/watch?v=8AB_4xKKOyM

A page: A large, golden menorah is encased near the Western Wall. Above left: A sign of peace and the Prince of Peace at the church in Bethlehem. Above right: Flowers bloom at a garden in Capernaum.

Above left and right: Whether you're traveling with family, friends, or on your own, a trip to Israel is one you'll never forget!

written and shared over the Internet. Knowing that she lived in Malawi, and knowing the situation for many who live there, I wasn't sure what to say. I began to pray about how to respond to her email, thinking that I'd say, "I believe that God can make a way, but I'm sorry I can't help you myself." As soon as I said those words in my mind, however, I felt God say, "Yes, you can help her." I said, "No, I can't." He said, "Yes you can." I said, "No, I can't!"

I had been planning this trip to Israel for the past 3 years, and our whole family had been working and saving money so that my wife and I and our four oldest kids could go with us. We barely had enough money at that time for just one of us to go, let alone six. So when God said

I could help Esther get there, too, I really didn't know what to do. So I wrote back to her and said simply that I believed God could make a way, and I'd be praying along with her.

As the summer went on, I kept reading the words of Jesus to His disciples from Matthew 14:13-21, when 5,000 people were gathered together on a hillside at dinnertime. Jesus told His disciples: "You give them something to eat." I could imagine what the disciples must have felt. They said that not even eight months wages would give everyone even one bite, so how could they feed them? All they had was five loaves of bread and two fish from a boy's lunch.

Yet I was puzzled why Jesus would ask them to do something impossible if He didn't think they could do it. didn't think they could possibly do. Unless, of course, they could do it, and they just didn't know how. I kept asking God, "How? How did Jesus do it? And how can we do it when You ask us to do something that seems impossible to us?"

So I studied that passage over and over, trying to see how Jesus did it. He simply gave thanks to God, broke the bread, and had the disciples start passing it out. Somehow there was enough food for all 5,000 to eat till they were satisfied and still have twelve baskets full left over.

As I shared this dilemma one week with a youth group, some of them came up to me afterwards and said they'd like to help with Esther's ticket. I tried to decline their money, because I didn't want them to think I was telling them the story in order for them to give money for the trip. I was just sharing with them the puzzle of how to do what God asks us to do when we think it is impossible. Several of them insisted, however, saying that they felt God really wanted them to give the money to help with Esther's trip. By the end of that week, I had received just over $300—enough to make the deposit on the trip for Esther to come with us. But I still needed more than 10 times that amount to pay for her whole trip, plus I still had to pay for my own family to go. I didn't tell Esther about the money yet, nor the deposit. I just told her that I was still praying for her, and asked if she could get her passport information to me in case God were to make a way for her to come with us.

As the trip got closer, I just couldn't let go of the idea that God wanted me to help Esther get to Israel, but I still didn't know how. So I sent out a note to some others who also read my weekly devotionals on the Internet, letting them know about the situation. We received about a third of the total needed for her trip from that appeal. Another man donated about a third of the cost to cover her airfare from Malawi, and Lana and I put in the final third, as God was also working at the same time to help the six of us going from our family to pay for our trips, too. I told Esther the good news, that God had made a way for her to join us. By the time we left, everyone's ticket was completely paid for! This was astounding!

But then we got to Israel. We were supposed to meet Esther at the airport, as she was to arrive on a flight about twelve hours earlier. But when we got there, we couldn't find her. We paged her several times over the airport intercom, we checked for phone messages and email messages, looked in all the waiting areas, but couldn't find anything about where she might be, or if she even made it on

Below: My wife's favorite drink in Israel (or anywhere!): freshly-squeezed pomegranate juice, as sold here on the street near the the Tower of David Museum.

Above: A memorial at Yad Vashem to the children who died in the Holocaust .

her flights. We finally had to leave the airport, knowing that I had at least sent her the names of the hotels where we'd be staying at before we left, and hoped that she would catch up with us.

But she didn't. She called us the next day from an airport in Addis Ababa, Ethiopia. Although she had made it all the way to the airport in Israel, they had denied her entry into Israel, saying that it was too questionable about how she came to know us through our Internet ministry,

and why the rest of the group wasn't there to meet her in Israel when she arrived. Although she tried to explain it to them several times, and she was even still in the airport when our flight finally landed twelve hours later, she wasn't allowed to call or email or make any contact with us. (To the credit of the airport security in Israel, they run a very tight ship and for very good reasons. We appreciate that they take their job so seriously or otherwise no one would be able to travel in and around Israel at all.) But since Esther did not travel together with us into the country with the group, she was questioned more strictly and finally put on a plane, headed back to her home.

I couldn't believe it when she told me the story over the phone and I began trying to think of anything else I could do. We had come too far in getting her to this point that I didn't want to give up on it, even though she was already headed on her flights back home, now waiting in Ethiopia to change planes back to Malawi. I called the immigration office at the Addis Ababa airport to ask if she could be put back on the plane to Israel, that we would meet her at the airport when she arrived and try to provide whatever documents they needed to verify that she was on our tour, but they said there was nothing they could do for her. She had been officially deported, and they were to put her on a flight back to Malawi the next morning. After several calls to several different people at the immigration office, I couldn't get any farther. I went to bed that night wondering why God had brought her so far, only to have her turned back in the end. It was 4 in the morning by this time, and I couldn't think of anything else to do, so I finally slept.

When I woke up a few hours later, I updated my wife Lana on the situation,

and asked if she could think of anything else we could do. She remembered that a friend of ours had a daughter who had just come home from serving a year in Ethiopia as a missionary, and maybe she would have a contact who could help us out. I didn't know what they could even do, but I felt I had to pursue any possible option that was still open to us, as I felt it was the Lord who had put it on my heart to try to get her there in the first place. So we texted our friend's daughter back in Chicago, who texted us back with the phone number of a pastor she knew in Addis Ababa. I was astounded that we knew someone who knew someone who lived in Addis Ababa at all!

And I couldn't believe it when we called him and he immediately said that he would do whatever we needed him to do, just let him know. It was such a surprise that my wife and I both cried at the thought that someone would take a call from complete strangers and would be

Right: For cat lovers reading this book, here's one more parting shot of the many cats of Israel!

Above: Photographers Karis Elder (left) and Makari Elder (right), with our excellent local Israeli guide, Pilar Blanco (center).

the whole trip, and they said they could try to fax a letter to immigration in Addis Ababa, saying that Esther was indeed part of our tour, and that she was an invited guest as part of our group. I called the immigration office again, saying that we'd try to get a letter to them if they could just let Esther stay at the airport another 5-6 hours, as it was the middle of the night back in the States, and the tour offices wouldn't be open yet for another several hours. They granted our request and didn't make her get on the next-scheduled flight to Malawi.

So we got their fax number and the tour company tried several times to fax the letter—but the fax wouldn't go through. As the day went on, the rest of our group in Israel continued on with our tour, now sitting in a garden in the city of Capernaum, a site where Jesus had done some incredible miracles. I updated the group on Esther's situation, and we all prayed that someone would be able to get that letter through to the immigration office. I didn't have the heart to call the pastor in Addis Ababa again, but Lana did, so she tried to call him. None of her calls would go through. We sat down again and prayed. Our time was running out.

At the very moment that we sat down to pray, my phone rang. It was the pastor from Addis Ababa! He said he had just

willing to drop everything and go to the airport right away. He was a busy man with a large congregation and they had just gotten out of some special weekday services they were holding. It was beyond what we could have imagined someone doing for us in this situation. It still makes me cry to think of it—a brother in Christ willing to help out another brother, simply because we have the same Father. So he went to the airport that night, along with a pilot friend from his congregation. Unfortunately they weren't able to find Esther there. We were all disappointed, but we didn't know what else to do.

In the mean time, I had also talked to the tour company who helped us arrange been to the airport again to try one more time to find Esther, taking some of his church members with him, this time one who worked at the airport. They had found Esther! They were calling us to see if there was any possibility we could fax him a letter from the tour company saying that she was with our trip! It was the very thing we were trying to do, but he didn't know it, and I didn't know he had gone back to the airport again! I called the tour company who found a way to finally email to the pastor, who printed it out and took it back to the immigration office at the airport. I also instructed the tour company that if they needed to buy another ticket for Esther to get back to Israel, to go ahead and buy it and charge it to my account, up to $1,000, withhout having to try to call me. We didn't have time to wait for any more calls. I just wanted the ticket waiting for her at the airport if she needed it. I didn't have $1,000 to spend on her ticket, but that's the number that came into my mind while I was on the phone, and what I felt I should say.

The pastor was able to get the documents to Esther, and the immigration office said she could get on a

Below: The ruins at Beit She'an, one of the ten cities of the Decapolis, and the site of the entire filming of the movie *Jesus Christ, Superstar*.

Above: Our whole group, finally all together, in front of the Church of the Holy Sepulchre. Back row (left to right): Joe Gerstung, Ron Ballard, Craig Elder, Lucas Elder. Middle row: Esther Gondwe, Jeanette Gaylord, Karis Elder, Leanne Benner. Front row: Eric Elder, Lana Elder, Wayne Pogue, Josiah Elder (front), Makari Elder, Gary Marini, and Makayla Gaylord.

Esther wasn't yet back in Israel, I felt like I had done the utmost of what I could possibly do to get her to Israel, as God had called me to do.

The next morning, our first stop on our tour "just happened" to be the site where Jesus multiplied the loaves and the fish to feed the 5,000—the place where Jesus had told the disciples to give the people something to eat, and the passage which had so inspired me all along. There we were standing on the same hill where that miracle from God took place. As I was looked up the passage again to read to our group that morning, I saw that it was told in several of the gospels, so I looked at each version to see which one to read. When I read John's version of the story, I couldn't believe it! In his version, when Jesus asked Philip where they could get food for all these people to eat, John added:

"He asked this only to test him, for he already had in mind what He was going to do" (John 6:6).

plane back to Israel. The tour company agency found the cheapest ticket they could—it was $992, just $8 under the limit I had given them, so they bought it and had it waiting for her at the airline counter.

As I went to bed that night, exhausted not only from the recent days' activities, but also from the months leading up to this moment, I went to lay down and felt God said, "You passed the test. Enjoy the rest of the trip." I wasn't sure exactly what test I had passed, but I was thankful that it was all working out. Even though

It was a test! And just as Jesus had tested the disciples by asking them to give the people something to eat,—when it seemed utterly impossible—God had tested me to help someone else in need when it seemed impossible, too. And God had told me the night before that I had passed the test. Hallelujah! And now He had brought me to the hillside where Jesus had given the disciples their test! God couldn't have spoken more clearly to me if He had appeared in front of my eyes!

Later that afternoon, Esther arrived again at the airport in Israel, and this time she was allowed to enter the country. (The security people at the airport had asked her, "Why have you come back again when someone who is deported isn't allowed to attempt to come back into the country again for five years, and now you're trying to come back after only three days later!" Had I known that, I don't know that I would have even tried to get her back in. Only God could have opened that door for her to return!) She met us at the hotel for dinner that night.

Over dinner with our group, Esther and I shared with each other all that God had been doing to make this moment possible. And that's when the real clincher came.

Esther told me that from the very first day that I responded to her email, saying that I felt God could make a way for her to visit Israel someday, she said God spoke to her and told her she'd be coming this year, with us. Even when she was being turned away at the airport, she said she was praising God, that those had been the best few days of her life so far. Her mom had even called

me during all of this to say that she wasn't discouraged, that they were just going to thank God in all things in order to shame the devil. Esther said that from the very beginning, when she first started thinking about the trip, she wanted to pray that God would make a way for her to go, but that God had stopped her from praying. She said that God told her not to pray for the trip, but to simply give thanks for it. She was puzzled, but did what God said. In fact, as time went on she was tempted to ask others to start praying for her to be able to go on the trip, too, but that God had stopped her from telling even one person about the trip or to pray for her, but simply to continue to give thanks for

Below: Lucas says he got his first kiss in Israel....from a fish served for dinner at the Dead Sea.

Left: Another long day of touring comes to a sweet end.

felt that she had passed her test, too, because of her obedience. We both knew that while God would still use the rest of the trip to speak to us in many ways, that He had already done His greatest work in us already, that of increasing our faith in Him.

As if to confirm all that had just happened that day, when I got back to my hotel room that night and having shared all of this with Esther—even the part about authorizing the purchase of her second ticket for anything up to $1,000 when I didn't know how I'd be able to pay for it —I checked my email before heading for bed. In my inbox was a note saying that a friend of ours back in the States had unexpectedly made an online donation of $1,000 to our ministry while we were at dinner that night! It was as if God were putting the icing on the cake, covering even the final detail of her trip.

I still don't know how to interpret it all. On the one hand, it seems it wouldn't have happened had we not prayed fervently and worked feverishly towards the goal, even day and night near the end. But on the other hand, God wanted to teach us something through what He called Esther to do: to simply give thanks for what He was going to give her. Or as my wife said while we were going through the whole ordeal, she felt that we were like the workers who helped to dig Hezekiah's tunnel to bring water into the City of

it. She said she didn't feel she was supposed to tell anyone about the trip until it was set. When she got my email asking for her passport information, and before I had even told her that people had begun to give money for her to come, she said she knew on that day that everything was set, and she could finally begin telling others about it.

I was stunned by what she said. Wasn't that exactly what Jesus did on the hillside when He multiplied the loaves and the fish? He simply gave thanks to God, broke the bread, and asked the disciples pass it out. He didn't plead for it, He just gave thanks for it! I looked at Esther and thanked her for being obedient to what God had told her to do. It had spoken volumes to me, answering a question that had been on my heart for months as I studied that passage trying to see what Jesus had done. I told her what God said to me about passing the test, and that I

David. One team started digging from one side, and the other team started digging from the other side, and miraculously both teams were able to meet in the middle to complete the tunnel!

In any case, I hope that God will speak to you through at least some portion of this story. And for some reason, I don't think this is the end of the story. It could very well be the beginning of some new ones! Thanks again for joining us on this incredible trip to the Holy Land!

Let's pray:

Father, thank You for all the remarkable things we've learned from this trip to the Holy Land, and all the remarkable things you still want us to learn in the future. Give us the faith to step out and trust you completely for everything in our lives, giving You thanks, even in advance, for Your love and faithfulness to us. Thank You for sending Your Son to lead us in Your ways, and keep giving us the faith we need to follow Him every day, until one day He leads us on into heaven. In Jesus' name, Amen.

Below: A picture of Eric Elder, Esther Gondwe, and Lana Elder, overlooking the Southern Steps of the Temple Mount, where Jesus often taught His followers to put their full faith and trust in God. Back page: A reminder from the Garden Tomb to pray for the peace of Jerusalem (Psalm 122:6).

PRAY for the PEACE of JERUSALEM

CPSIA information can be obtained
at www.ICGtesting.com
Printed in the USA
LVOW03s2004251215
467860LV00003B/78/P